WORKERS' PARTICIPATION IN MANAGEMENT IN POLICY MAKING

WORKERS' PARTICIPATION IN MANAGEMENT IN POLICY MAKING

PRAGMATIC CASE STUDIES

ABHINAV KUMAR SHRIVASTAVA

PARTRIDGE
A Penguin Random House Company

To order additional copies of this book, contact
Partridge India
000 800 10062 62
orders.india@partridgepublishing.com

www.partridgepublishing.com/india

CONTENTS

LIST OF FIGURES

LIST OF DIAGRAMS

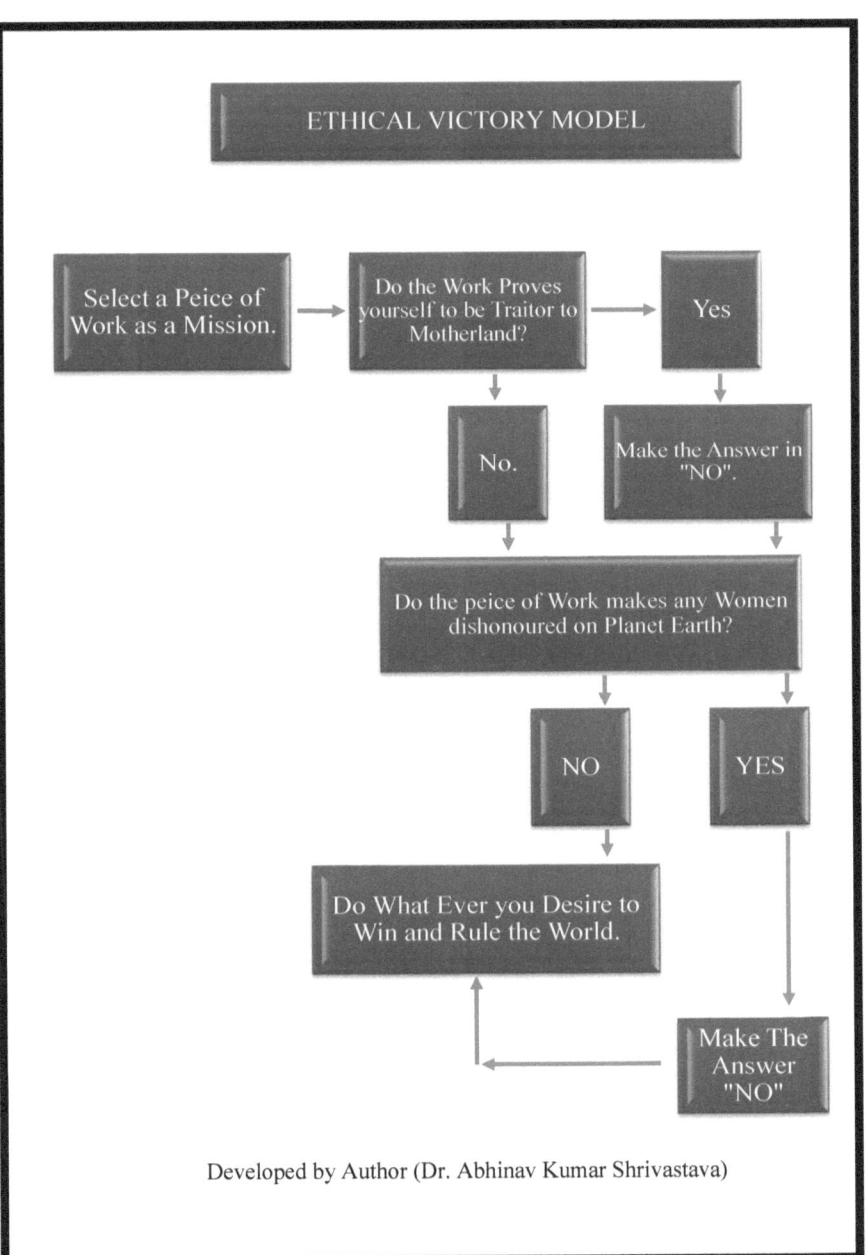

Developed by Author (Dr. Abhinav Kumar Shrivastava)

Developed by Author (Dr. Abhinav Kumar Shrivastava)

RATIONALE BEHIND THE PROPOSED ETHICAL VICTORY MODEL

I am "Gallant Proud" to be an Indian. As an Indian I believe in texts of Sacred Veds which recites "**Jatra Pujyate Nari, Tatra Ramte Dev**". It explains that where women are worshiped, honored and are safe and always are given top priority there only God resides. And where God resides there is always prosperity, peace and happiness.

The last Chapter of the Greatest Epic in World, The Mahabharta there is a scene describing the last teaching of Bhism to his grandsons and Lord Krishna. Bhism says "Peace and Prosperity depends only on two factors. The first is the boundaries of protection of Motherland and second is Honor of Women. Any empire can only flourish where women are respected, are safe and are protected from even the minor odds. No society can progress toward prosperity without welfare and protection of women". Bhism also instructed to his grandsons and Lord Krishna and shared "Janani(Mother) chhah(and) Janambhumi(Motherland), Prathemaey (Prior to) Sthaney(Position) Swarge(Heaven)". It means a universal dictum that "Position of Mother and Motherland is even more prior to heaven. The outmost honor, care and protection have to be given to Mother and Motherland". And with these "*Golden Historical Words*" Bhisma sacrificed his life.

Lord Shiv is known as the god who can defeat death. Shiv in Hindi is written as "शिव"

and the "Feminine Hindi Language's Phonetics" is removed then it become Shav "शव".

And Shav means Dead Body in Hindi Language. So if a woman touches even a man then from a dead body he turns into a Lord Status. As per ancient Hindu mythology Goddess "Kali Maa" (Mother Kali) has kept her feet over chest of Lord Shiv in order to combat the demons. And Lord Shiv gracefully surrendered himself at foots of Goddess Kali. So women are historically respectable.

Lord Krishna is another Lord in Hindu mythology who is respected a lot. The major reason was his bold confrontation against women discrimination and to help Draupadi to provide her clothes while she (Draupadi) was sexually harassed and that too in public domain. Till today during Holi in Mathura, where Krishna was born, first the males must get beaten by women and then if a woman wishes then only women can put colors first over men. And men must follow all decorum and laws while playing colors.

In ancient India, the ritual of "**Swayamvar**" was given only to women where she was free to choose her life partner. But today the "**Masculine-Dominated**" mindset has created hostile environment for women all around world.

As an Ethical Common Indian I decided to progress ahead with keeping the same factors in my mind. And after a deep research I found a mid way to overcome all obstacles in path of progress. And I made a healthy attempt to shape "***Ethical Victory Model***". By the same model my Motherland my "***Mother India***" and honor of all women of world are secured and protected. All women all around the world in my mindset points for every women without any discrimination on basis of caste, creed, region, religion, demography, race, nationality, ethnicity.

My Mother and all women around the world face the same Labor Pain while birth of the child. And with bearing such an enormous pain the generations continues on planet earth.

As a graduate in History I skimmed a deep research and found that, in a global context the most of the parts of World has been ruled by the "***British Crown***", "***Mongolian Empire***" and the "***Ottoman Empire***". The British Rule gave birth of colonial culture and a well framed administrative set up to its ruled colonies all around world. While the Mongolian Empire has given the "***Silk Route***" to world and the "***Ottoman Empire***" reshaped the mindset of masses for ***pro democracy*** resulting into transfer of powers within Turkey to the Grand National Assembly of Turkey. Also the Ottoman Empire was having control on maximum of sea connecting coasts of Asia, Europe and African sub continent. These all factors made the Ottoman rule one of the most powerful and prosperous kingdoms in world at a time.

But switching duration of fall of power control from supreme glory heights to dwelling of sunset for the "***Mongolian Empire***" to the "***Ottoman Empire***" was observed only between 4-5 years of duration of time.

The *"Mongolian Empire"* started uprising in 1206 AD and started decline in 1332 AD, while the *"Ottoman Empire"* emerged from 1299 AD to 1922 AD. While on other hand the "East India Company" scaled the globe in one joint and a time came that their sun never set all around the day for the Company.

If we closely watch then we find that the Mongolian Empire took brilliant expansion in a very short period of time by invading the tribes and local population. But initially during expansion the rulers, yes of course they use to settle with local community after marriage negotiations and bargains to marry local girls, widows of soldiers of the enemy. Many time they also exercised forced marriage as well as multiple marriages. But **_no records_** are found where the Mongols have harassed or made any harm to the Women.

The Mongolian rulers believed in Personal exchange in form of medicine, knowledge, technology, agriculture, cuisine and other commodities with local people in order to consolidate and expand their ruling canvas. These factors created a mutual trust between the Empire and the followers of Empire as the followers were no having feeling of security against any form of harassment of women.

The Mongols also unlocked the "Silk Route" which gave the new shape to global economy. Many records prove that between 1292 AD to 1310 AD countless sexual assault on women, rapes and brutal torture to innocent girls was performed by Mongol Invaders. In a concise the *"Gender Atrocity"* was the prime cause of revolt resulting into downfall and rapid collapse of *"Mongolian Empire"*. By 1332 Mongol Empire it was at almost on verge of being extinct.

While exploring the last days of the Ottoman Empire it has been recorded with facts and proofs that the *"**Molestation**"* of women, *"**Sexual slavery**"* was at much higher rate in Ottoman society in its last decades of rule. The practice carried over into complete Ottoman reign. As late as 1902, female slaves were sold in the Ottoman Empire.

These factors accelerated the business of *"**Woman Trafficking**"* of innocent women. And was one of the prime causes of revolt against the incumbent rulers and political leaders. As in any religion the harassment of woman is a very big sin. Gradually the *"**Ottoman Empire**"* also collapsed.

While in my opinion, The Great British Empire never saw sunset with Supreme rule with glory all over the world, because the highest authority was given to women. Further it is also a beautiful secret that the world's costliest and largest diamond the "Kohi-Noor" has a bad luck which does not affect women only. And if any masculine who owned the "Kohi-Noor" Diamond will surely face disaster, and for the same it was placed at Crown of "British Queen" who ruled the world.

On the other hand if we see life of Rani Laxmi Bai, she sacrificed her life as a martyr and ordered her body to be cremated by her own followers. Her own soldiers performed the sacred rituals after her supreme sacrifice to protect her mother land. The martyr of Rani Laxmi Bai was a chosen option of "Honor Supreme Sacrifice" for protection of Motherland, it was not any form of harassment to a women by British. Twenty years after her death Colonel Malleson wrote in the *History of the Indian Mutiny*; vol. 3; London, 1878 "Whatever her faults in British eyes may have been, her countrymen will ever remember that she was driven by ill-treatment into rebellion, and that she lived and died for her country".

Eventually after the brutal massacre of "Jalilianwala Bagh" on instructions of Colonel **Reginald Edward Harry Dyer,** on **April 13, 1919 AD** the British Sun started to dip down. And Great Britain lost their largest and wealthiest colony, "India" in less than three decades of time. And later in just less than half a century The British Crown lost its maximum colonies.

My view says that the fall of British Rule in India was due to negative impact of atrocity on women at Jalliawala Bagh massacre and later many more. As British used Gun Power to establish Colonial rule in India since 1857. But they never directly tortured women. Even the British Rulers has a lot of respect for Rani Laxmi Bai.

Parallel to this, in 1927 during the Sino-Japanese war the powerful Imperial Japanese Army created **"Nanking Massacre",** where Women from age of six months to Ninety Years were targeted. About 400000 (Four Hundred Thousand) women brutally Gang raped in just six weeks. After Gang rapes, Women they were nude paraded and later they were either cut into pieces or victim's private part was pierced with knife of any sharp weapon.

The Imperial Japanese Army forced to exercise "Incest Rapes" over victims. Father were forced to rape their daughter, Son were Forced to rape their Mother, Grandfather was forced to Rape their minor innocent granddaughter and grandson were forced to rape their caring old aged grandmothers, in order to save their Grand Mothers, Mothers, Daughters and granddaughters from Gang Rape and then nude parade to be done by Imperial Japanese Army.

Later the Imperial Japanese Army raped Grand Mothers, Mothers, Daughters and granddaughters who were already made victim of helpless rape by their Grandfather, Father, Brother and Sons, in a "hopeless hope" to save their women from Gang Rape and nude parade by Imperial Japanese Army.

I have no conflict with Government of Japan. As any Government cannot be blamed for the power being misused by their authorities. Also I don't want to elaborate any more the atrocities on women exercised by Imperial Japanese Army during Sino-Japanese War.

My personal view says that it was result of same "***Rape Genocide***" that Japan faced **"Historical Curse"** of Nuclear Attacks on 06th August 1945 and 09th August 1945 was an Ethical curse of "**Nanking Massacre**" that till today there is adverse radioactive radiation effect affecting the lives of people of Japan. I pray that accidents as **"Nanking Massacre"** and **"Nuclear Attack on Japan"** may never happen again. As these accidents are curse on human race. Unethical deeds of few people results into graze to millions of innocent life.

In a complex situation, another question also comes in mind that what to do if a women is culprit in heinous crimes? Then let me share my opinion to punish such woman. And my experience says that such culprit woman must be punished lawfully, legally with maintaining decorum and protocols so that her honor and modesty may not be even minor harmed. Generally if required then the issue must be handled by women only, which is a common practice is major progressive democratic countries all around the globe.

In a composite gist I can say the real "Gender Empowerment" can only be done with making provision of honor, safety and security initially in our mindsets and then also in social environment. I believe teachings of Mahatma Ghandhi "Be the change in system, what you want see the change in system". So let us begin the change with change in our mindset at initial stage.

Every woman whom I don't know, for me is my "Lekhan Preyasi". The word "Lekhan Preyasi" has been derived from ancient Indian Sanskrit Texts and it means a "***Beautiful Sacred Woman***" who is being viewed with outmost honor by writer and motivates the writer to script something very innovative and constructive. The "***Lekhan Preyasi***" is always being seen from a distance and it is said that "***No touch***" can be made to "***Lekhan Preyasi***" by the writer. As if the writer touches the "***Lekhan Preyasi***" then "***Lekhan Preyasi***" vanishes out as if someone would have touched a "***Sacred soft bubble***"!!.

It is believed that "***Lekhan Preyasi***" is "***Sacred Ink-Pot***" of the writer and smile of "***Lekhan Preyasi***" is "***Sacred Ink with Spiritual Essence***". The imagination of writer is remarked as its "***Writing Pen***". And if the "***Sacred Ink-Pot***" don't have ink or the "***Sacred Ink-Pot***" vanishes out then writer is helpless with his "***Barren Pen***" without "***Ink with Spiritual Essence***."

I hereby grant my authorization all my respected readers of this book that they can convert the gist of this "***Ethical Victory Model***" in any language and translate as per their requirements.

As I want to disseminate my views as a view of an "***Indian***" to every corner of world. I request all my readers to please feel free to add upon on my proposed concept. I am making this declaration so that there may not be any charges of "***Plagiarism***" over any person.

As I am too much "***Ambitious Person***" to establish myself as an "***Ethical and Aggressive Entrepreneur***" so I will strictly follow "***Ethical Victory Model***". And I recommend that all other must also think over it to be followed.

The logic behind this proposed concept of "***Ethical Victory Model***" in this book of Workmen's issue is to disseminate the concept to maximum. As this model is relevant in every human being's life.

I admit my mistake that my vocabulary, phonetics and grammar are extremely poor and much weak. I apologies in anticipation for all forms of errors and mistakes made by me while narrating this complete book.

I extend my humble request to all the readers for their valuable feedbacks for improvement in my future academic assignments.

Best Regards,
Dr. Abhinav Kumar Shrivastava
(The Foolest Human on Planet Earth)

ACKNOWLEDGEMENT

I take this opportunity to extend my disciplined thanks to my PhD thesis supervisor Prof (Dr) N.C.Pahariya for his guidance and mentoring in successful completion of my research exploration of my PhD Thesis topic. With kind guidance and motivation of Prof (Dr) N.C.Pahariya Sir my ambition propagated to shape my Ph.D Thesis in form of a rich academic text book.

I extend my sincere thanks to GM (HRD), BCCL, Kalyan Bhawan Dhanbad for kind grant of permission to complete my training of PhD research work. I also extend my sincere thanks to all personnel of Personnel Directorate, BCCL, Koyla Bhawan Dhanbad

I also express my sincere thanks to Mr. A. Abeygunasekera, Secretary, Ministry of Water supply and Drainage, Government of Sri Lanka, for his kind permission to complete the Research Project for data collection of my PhD Research work at Ministry of Water supply and Drainage, Government of Sri Lanka and also at National Water Supply and Drainage Board of Sri Lanka.

I express my sincere gratitude to Mrs. Chandika V. Ethugala, Director Development, Ministry of Water supply and Drainage, Government of Sri Lanka, who guided us with rich literature material available for Sustainable usage of water.

I express my thanks to Ms. Tanuja Ariyananda, Executive Director, Lanka Rain Water Harvesting Forum, Nugegoda Sri Lanka for her kind help to made us acquaint with most modern method for Rain water conservation.

I would also like to extend my sincere gratitude to my professional senior Dr.S.S.Chawhan, Vice-Principal, Institute of Management and Computer Science, NIMS University, Shobhanagar, Jaipur for his kind help in collection of data related to my PhD research topic.

I also extend my sincere thanks to Dr(Mrs) Jaswant Sokhi, Faculty of School of Life Sciences, I.G.N.O.U. for providing key resource literature from knowledge bank of E-Gyankosh of I.G.N.O.U. which enabled me to frame rich literature review for my Ph.D Thesis.

I extend my humble thanks to Honorable Editorial board of IJRCM, IJCSMS for their kind grant of permission to convert my published papers in editions of journals. Without their kind support it was an uphill task for me complete this book.

Before I may stop I once again extend my sincere thanks to my PhD thesis supervisor Prof (Dr) N.C.Pahariya Sir for his kind mentoring and guidance.

Dr. Abhinav Kumar Shrivastava
Date: - 19 August, 2014.
Place:- Dhanbad, State of Jharkhand,
Republic of India.

GRATITUDE FOR CARE TAKER OF OUR FAMILY THE COAL INDIA LIMITED COMPANY

I remember July of year 1989 when I first started visiting Jyoti School Jayant. At every 10:30 we little kids in school, use to hear the siren of safety and at every 12:55 pm we use to hear the final safety siren before the blast. In next few minutes between 1:05 pm to 1:15 pm we use to feel our body vibrated due to heavy blasting in mines. And with the final clearance of mines for "Accident Free" blasting us also get rings of school to go home.

Jumping in typical Soviet model of huge size "School Buses" we use to reach home. And generally me and all kids use to find their heroic Dad washing their painted face and taking bath with warm water to remove coal dust from their body. In next ten minutes we all use to sit for lunch with our families. And with finishing of lunch we use to go to sleep or play.

But by next two three hour we find many of our Uncles and even many times my Dad getting again ready for the evening shift or night shift duty in working coal mines. As this is the typical culture of "Hot Seat" culture of twenty four hour operative coal mines.

I remember five days of lunch with my father, then dinner without him. Later five days dinner with father but no breakfast or lunch with him, and finally breakfast with him then no lunch or dinner with him. Once in a month when Dad use to get Giant rest after a fortnight then I remember to have breakfast, lunch and dinner with him.

This cyclic story is common for every family in Coal India. I am thankful to Coal India Limited Company for providing job opportunities to more than 1.5 million people in past 30 years and also being a backbone support to the Energy Sector in India.

Every personnel who works in Coal India Limited is cared for his four generations by the company. The first is the Parents of Employee, second is employee herself/himself, and third is the offspring of the employee. Definitely the fourth is offspring's next generation, who is born in a well groomed environment.

If we count one generation to live for sixty years of life, then one personnel in Coal India is secure for future two generations resulting into a secured future for next 180 years. This is my calculation!!

I also dedicate my disciplined tribute to all my Uncles who sacrificed their precious life while serving the Company and combating the disaster to save life of their colleagues. As the "Nature of mining is against Nature", due to the same many disastrous conditions as accidents, natural calamity are to be face by brave working personnel in Coal India Limited company all around the day, week, month, years....

The resonance of beautiful echo buzzing of blasting in mines and the Essence of Fragrance of Black Diamond (Coal) was felt by me since I was in embryo stage safely inside safeguard cover womb of my Mother.

I have taken the very realistic basic case studies to shape it into absolute practical case studies so that the real outcomes can be expressed. The theoretical knowledge has a limit and with sharing more practical spheres definitely the coming generations will turn more advanced and filtered to make tremendous developments toward a prosperous Economic state.

There are many more things to share about Coal India Limited Company. But lack of time and space doesn't permit me to write more.

Love you too much, our "Parent Company", Our Coal India Limited Company!!

Dr. Abhinav Kumar Shrivastava
Date: - 19 August, 2014.
Place:- Dhanbad, State of Jharkhand,
Republic of India.

ETHICAL THANKS

I extend my discipline thanks to my "Respected Teachers". As Maa is my First Teacher and Father is my first mentor. And My First Teachers has always taught me to give outmost respect to my Academic Teachers and to see an image of Guardian in them.

*It my personal opinion that **"Real Victory** of a Parent and Teacher is at the moment when they are superseded by their child" And I am well assured that soon I will be achieving **"Real Victory"** for my Parents and Teachers. Life is a relay race where the older generations transfer the lightening lamp in safe hands of new generations, and new generations has to move ahead with pace, dedication and Excellence.*

I also extend my sincere thanks to my elder brother Dr. Abhishek Kumar Shrivastava for his support throughout my life.

My microscopic level of knowledge doesn't permit to write more.

Dr. Abhinav Kumar Shrivastava
Date: - 19 August, 2014.
Place:- Dhanbad, State of Jharkhand,
Republic of India.

FEW WORD FOR MY FRIENDS
OF THE JOURNEY

It's a life time emotional bond with my childhood friends Varsha(Nikki), Munna(Manish:-Our Thin Bread Slice), Md. Azharuddin, Abu Abraham, Raman Saket, Praven Mishra, Harman(Dimpi), Sachin Malik(Jaat Bhai of Merrut and my schoolmate), Parul Singh, Chintu(Avnish Singh), Bhanu Bhaiya, Garima Bhabhi, Ruby(Golgappi), Chandrashekhar Azad, Navnet Di, Namita Di, Anjuman, Rohan, Milton, Manish Sinha, Praveen (B.Pharma), Krishna Dev Bhaiya, Vivek Srivastava(N.C.L Khadiya), Babloo(Pradeep), Jaya, Samendra Bhaiya, Sandeep Bhaiya(Pilot), ILU, Dimpi, Golu-bholu, Tamma, Tangi, Prateek, Sonu, Gopu, Rahchit, Nehal, Anuraag and a few more whose face I remember but name I am missing as now it is more than a decades since I last met them.

At Indian School of Mines, only Satyndra Sinha as my first, last and best friend in MBA Department. Among my Professional seniors at MBA I extend my sincere thanks to Bishmbhar Sir, Shashank Sir, Anand Batta Sir, Tapan Sir, Radha Mam', Neetu Mam', Abhishek Singh Sir (M.Tech IE&M). Also Sachin Sharma, Chitalekha Mam', Sneha Gautam, Vikas Chatarjee, Rajneesh Srivastava from Environmental Department from ISM Dhanbad.

And a special thanks to Nishit Srivastava and President Sahab(Shailendra Boss), Satyanshu Srivastava, Shashank, Vikash Bagle, Tarique and all my colleagues and juniors of M.Tech(IE&M). I am highly obliged for their kind support and help in my academic journey.

Among my juniors of MBA I extend my sincere thanks to DK(Dilip), Vikash, Rahul Singh, Sandeep Sinha, Shrey, Vivek(LT) and most dear Nitish Srivastava.

During my Ph.D Curriculum I have learnt a lot from my Professional Seniors Dr. R.K.Sharma, Dr. S.S.Chawhan, Dr. Sandesh Sharma, Mr. Ruchir Saxena, Dr. Vikas Sharma, Dr. Akhil Goyal, Mrs. Savita Meel, Mr. Sonu Sharma, Mr. Nitin Vasu, Dr. Umendra Gaud, Dr. Vineeta Singh, Mr. Neeraj Gogia, Chanadni Mam', Dr. Arun Sharma, Mr. Ankit Baliyan (Balli Pra Jee), Aparna

Mam', Mr. Madhuram Kulshrestha, Mr. Tapan Pandya, Mr. Atul Pandey, Mr. KhemRaj Naruka, Mr. S.K.Verma, Surendra Jee(Accountant), Dr. Sayad (P.G. Scholar at NIMS Medical College). At the end, I am too much thankful to my only bacthmate in Ph.D course curriculum, Ms. Parul Jain for her kind help and moral support in my tough days of my health concern.

Now let me say a few words of appreciation for my disciplined students. I take this opportunity to share the disciplined planning of two of my good students. Raj Kamal Upadhyaya and Sunny (from Motihari, Bihar), who turned to be my two most faithful pillar in my International Research Explorations. I remember I was in rigor field assignment and I got an opportunity to apply for Visit to Sri Lanka. It was impossible for me to get even a single day's leave as well as the deadline for application was very nearby.

It was the brilliant coordination of Raj Kamal Upadhyaya and Sunny who got my all official documents approved in an extreme confidential manner by my Ph.D Thesis Supervisor Prof(Dr) N.C.Pahariya Sir within a working week.

It was the punctuality of both of my Power Swords (Raj and Sunny) that my approval came in less than one month from date of application from an International Academic Desk.

I extend my best wishes to Mrs. Namrata Ajit Mishra, Sayad Abuzar, Anajli Acharya, Vaishali Parmar, Meenakshi Agarwal, Gaurav Rawat, Janak Pandaya, Jyoti, Shreya, Parmindar, Rahul Yadav, and all my disciplined students of MBA Programme for their outmost disciplined regards for me.

I also extend my best wishes to Murari Gupta(MBA Intg), Udit Dubey (MBA Intg), Randhir Chaudhry (MBA Intg), Shyam Mishra(BBA), Ankita Suman(BBA) and most lovely "PAM (Parminder Pra)".

I feel privilege to say thanks to my three good students for their rock standing support against political conspiracy created for me by some unethical higher authorities. I say my proctored thanks to Vandana (BBA Intg), Jyoti(MBA) and Rahul Yadav(Lawyer), as these three students came to me and expressed their faith in me and encouraged me to fight for justice and assure me that at least they both are there in my support. It was the leadership attribute of these three brave students which gave inner motivation to me to continue to struggle against injustice. And later a huge mob of students, especially girl students rose in my support within 12 hours by following these three students. And within next 2-3 working days the problem against me was diffused and I emerged as an ethical winner. I sincerely extend my thanks to these three students.

Let me share me the real contribution of three of my key students who are equal to my family members. My three "Family Students" Vikash(Vickey), Vipul, Mannii (Manish), all students of BCA Programme. My three friends has prepared three times meals for me and has given me warm hospitality in my transit stay at their residence as well as continuous stay for about three months in last phase of my Ph.D Thesis submission.

It was these three student's sacrifice of comfort, that even in bone freezing chill of winter at Jaipur I continued uninterrupted in my finishing last moment hectic thread ware works of my Ph.D Thesis submission.

I remember my younger brothers Nitin(sonu), Sudhakar(Sidhu), Kanu Pyara, Rananjay, Rangesh, Patel Bhai(B.Pharma), Amlendu, Manvendra Gaurav, Rohit(Library), Abid, Deepesh, Nirbhay Mathur, Suman Paul, Rangesh, Himanshu, Kapil Sharma (MBBS), Shubhit agarwal, Rahul Ameta(Golu), Gagan Jain, and all my younger brothers whose name face I remember and name is again missing from mind!!

In my Ph.D Project My best Friend at NIMS University, Mr. Chandan Hait (B.Tech Bio-Technology) spent countless hours even in his hectic schedule in identifying and removing vocabulary errors in all my Ph.D Project related Data Collection.

In my last weeks at Jaipur I found a true gem as a Friend, Arun Panikkar Sir. I proudly say that I am lucky to have him as a friend in my life. At the end I feel proud to declare that I will be always emotionally bonded with Saroj Hostel, Achrol, Jaipur. The room which I hired as a renter was actually granted to me as a landlord. I am very thankful to Sharma Uncle Jee, the landlord of Hostel for making me felt delighted every moment.

Tea of Kalu Bhaiya, the caring and friendly behavior as a Family Friend of Nitin Sharma (Son of LandLord of Saroj Hostel) and everyone at Saroj Hostel.

I also extend my friendly thanks to Manish, the owner of Manish Infotech at Tambi Market, Achrol, Jaipur for his 24X7 support in maximum possible works.

If name of any of my friends would have been left out, then I apologize in anticipation.

Dr. Abhinav Kumar Shrivastava
Date: - 19 August, 2014.
Place:- Dhanbad, State of Jharkhand,
Republic of India.

CHAPTER#1

Introduction to Workers' Participation in Management.

As per Article 43 of Constitution of India [1,] the Living wage, etc, for workers, the State shall Endeavour to secure, by suitable legislation or economic organization or in any other way, to all workers, agricultural, industrial or otherwise, work, a living wage, conditions of work ensuring a decent standard of life and full enjoyment of leisure and social and cultural opportunities and, in particular, the State shall endeavor to promote cottage industries on an individual or co operative basis in rural areas.

COLLECTIVE BARGAINING

Collective bargaining [2] is process of joint decision making and basically represents a democratic way of life in industry. It is the process of negotiation between firm's and workers' representatives for the purpose of establishing mutually agreeable conditions of employment. It is a technique adopted by two parties to reach an understanding acceptable to both through the process of discussion and negotiation.

In order to create a safe working condition, workers should be allowed to participate actively in safety and health matters and cooperate with the employers. Since they are closer to their work, it is felt that the workers themselves are the most qualified to make decisions about safety and job improvements by exercising collective bargaining [3.]

THE COMPOSITE PROCESS OF COLLECTIVE BARGAINING

The collective bargaining is one of the most significant tools to empower the concept of WPM [4]. The complete process comprises of five core steps as follows (See Diagram 1):-

1. **Prepare**: This phase involves composition of a negotiation team consisting the representatives of both the parties with adequate knowledge and skills for negotiation.
2. **Discuss**: Here, the parties decide the ground rules that will guide the negotiations. A process well begun is half done and this is no less true in case of collective bargaining. An environment of mutual trust

and understanding is also created so that the collective bargaining agreement would be reached.

3. **Propose**: This phase involves the initial opening statements and the possible options that exist to resolve them. In a word, this phase could be described as 'brainstorming'. The exchange of messages takes place and opinion of both the parties is sought.

4. **Bargain**: negotiations are easy if a problem solving attitude is adopted. This stage comprises the time when 'what ifs' and 'supposals' are set forth and the drafting of agreements take place.

5. **Settlement:** Once the parties are through with the bargaining process, a consensual agreement is reached upon wherein both the parties agree to a common decision regarding the problem or the issue. This stage is described as consisting of effective joint implementation of the agreement through shared visions, strategic planning and negotiated change.

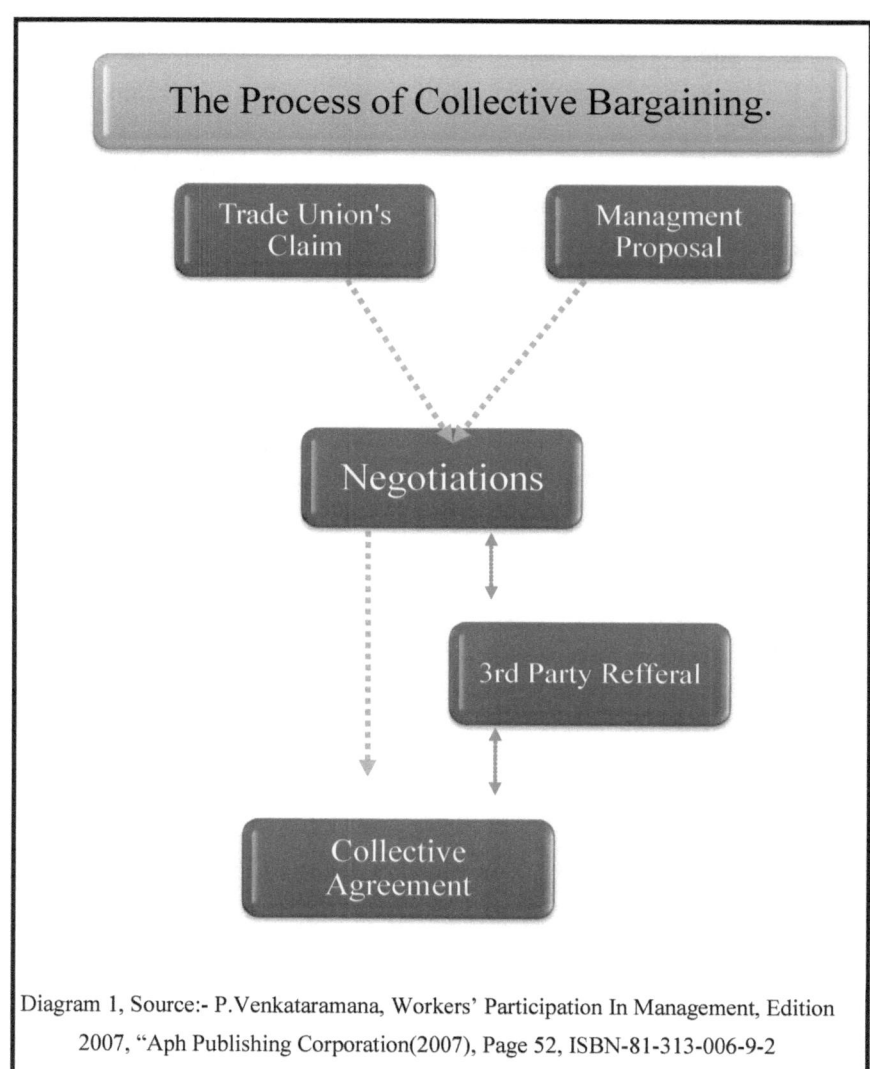

Diagram 1, Source:- P.Venkataramana, Workers' Participation In Management, Edition 2007, "Aph Publishing Corporation(2007), Page 52, ISBN-81-313-006-9-2

1) *Basu DD, Constitution of India, Tata McGraw Hills, 14th Edition, New Delhi, 2001, 32-33.*

2) *Datar BN, Participative management and Collective bargaining,* British Industrial Labour Journal, *UK, 1984; 9:17-20.*

3) *Dhingra OP, Participative predisposition's of public sector managers, Journal of Institute of Public Enterprises, Hyderabad, 1992; 8: 1201- 1211.*

4) *Micheal A. Landrun, Experiments with Workers' participation in the USA, Journal of Industrial Safety, USA, 1981;12: 143-145.*

CHAPTER#2

WPM Enhances Gender Empowerment

INTRODUCTION

The Coal India Company is the largest manpower employer in world in coal industry. The company is one of the five Maharatna Public Sector Undertaking Companies of Government of India. The Company have nine sister subsidiaries. And the coal reserves which are excavated are found in several states of India. And on these reserves the operating mines of Coal India is performing the coal production with decentralization of work by coordination of all the personnel working in nine sister subsidiaries. (Pl. refer Diagram 2)

The BCCL Company (Bharat Coking Coal Limited) is the world's largest Prime Coking Coal producing company as well as a NavRatna Company and the largest subsidiary in terms of manpower of the Maharatna Status Company **"Coal India Limited"**.

The BCCL company provides the high calorific value coal for Bokaro steel industry in nearby and also for The Chandrapura thermal power plant. Nationalization was done on **01.05.1972** brought under the **Bharat Coking Coal Limited BCCL**, a new Central Government Undertaking. Another enactment, namely the **Coal Mines Taking Over of Management Act, 1973**, extended the right of the Government of India to take over the management of the coking and non-coking coal mines in seven States including the coking coal mines taken over in 1971.

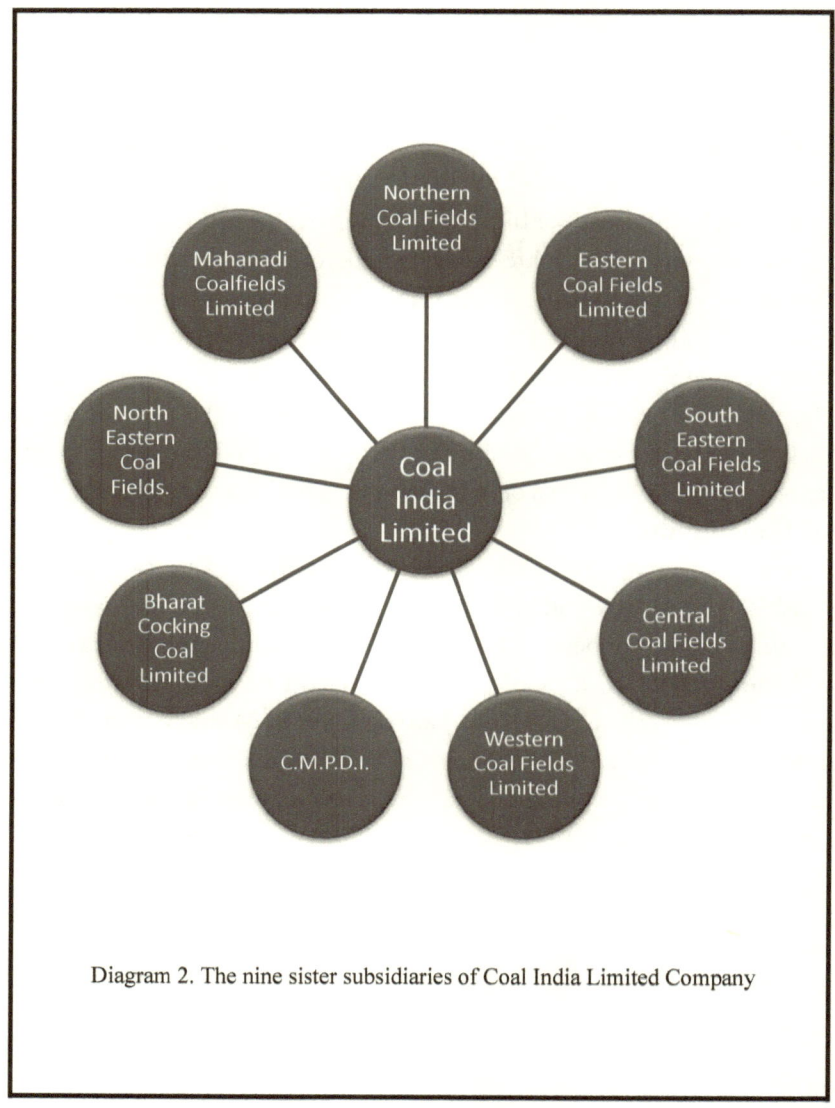

Diagram 2. The nine sister subsidiaries of Coal India Limited Company

PRACTICAL REAL CASE STUDY

An academic visit was by author made to Vocational Training Centre at Area-4 (Katras Area). The model of Gender empowerment by help of education and vocational training is common found in all the twelve working areas of the BCCL, Dhanbad. The visit was made to Area-4 as it is located at the prime coking coal belt of the BCCL Company as well as it is one of the biggest coal producing units among the sister units. For the same it is a big junction for generation of employment. Mr. Deenanath Prasad welcomed the author in a decent and warm manner and provided all forms of details permissible by law of company [2].

As well as the author was also taken to the running class to see in practical the classes being conducted for the Gender Empowerment. It was found that the women who work in the Bharat Coking Coal Limited Company were absorbed for education at Vocational Training Centre. A total of 60 days schedule is being provided to these women from initial training to final examination. Initially women personnel are given the basic education of alphabets and numbers. After two weeks they are taught with words, sentence forming and identification of symbols and colors being used in various discipline of working mines (Pl refer Figure 1).

A minimum basic education is imparted so that these women personnel can join the various departments in the Company within the permissible legal Industrial Acts and Legislative rules of Government of India.

The number of women in every batch counts generally 20-30. The women taking classes are the employees of Bharat Coking Coal Limited Company. And they have joined the company on basis of accidental compensation against their family members.

Figure 1. Author (Dr. Abhinav Kumar Shrivastava) interviewing Mr. Deenanath at Vocational Training Centre, BCCL Katras Area, Dhanbad, State of Jharkhand, Republic of India.

It was identified by author (Pl refer Figure 2) that these women, as a students use to perform their duty in their respective office every day. And after the initial hour's work they use to come to Vocational Training Centre for one hour to study. The women students are being granted a leave of 3 hours per day to attend the classes including their transit time for visit to Vocational Training Centre.

After being trained these feminine working personnel give their joining to various respective sections. Even they have proven themselves in the masculine handled portfolios of operating heavy earth moving mining machineries.

One of the precedence of Excellence is of Shri.Mamta Kumari of the "**Chetudih Colliery**" of Area-4 of BCCL Company, who won gold medal for her excellent performance in examination and now she is operating heavy dozers. Shri **Mamta Kumari** was awarded the memento of appraisal on occasion of "**Ghandhi Jayanti**" on 02nd October 2010 with kind presence by then acting Superintendent of Police of the Dhanbad District Mrs.Suman Gupta (I.P.S).

Even a few women have joined as electricians and mechanical personnel at pump stations for repairing and wiring of pressure pumps. As mentioned by Shri Deenanath Prasad that these arenas were untouched till date by women personnel.

Figure 2. Author (Dr. Abhinav Kumar Shrivastava) at Vocational Training Centre, Katras Area, Bharat Coking Coal Limited, Dhanbad, State of Jharkhand, Republic of India.

Many times it was reported that the illiterate widows were cheated by their own family relatives while withdrawing the money from their own bank account. As the value withdrawn were manipulated by their own trustworthy people without their knowledge.

But after being educated now these women can withdraw their own money by filling of the withdrawal form with their own. And also they are now well accustomed with digits and language to handle the ATM transactions (Automatic Teller Machine Transactions). This has been possible by education schemes t empower the working women personnel of BCCL, Dhanbad. (Pl refer Figure 3)

Figure 3. The special training and education programme for working women personnel at Vocational Training Centre, Kartras Area, Bharat Coking Coal Limited, Dhanbad, State of Jharkhand, Republic of India.

FINDINGS

It was found that out of 18 women personnel in first batch of gender empowerment initiatives taken by BCCL Company, the seventeen candidates passed the examination by first division and remaining one passed with second division. As told by Mr. Deenanath Prasad at present a total of 42(forty two) candidates has passed the Vocational Training successfully.

And in near future the strategy of BCCL company is to educate all the women candidates the computer proficiency. This is a planned strategy to be implemented soon so that more job avenues can be created in office works where women can perform duty in a proctored environment.

Mr. Deenanath Prasad also explained the simple mechanism of organizing this gender empowerment Vocational Training Programme. Initially a list of the candidates is made by the procedure of nomination from various departments of a running unit. And then it is forwarded by General Manager Chairperson of the working Unit to General Manager Chairperson of Human Resource Department of the BCCL Company.

Usually it takes duration of three to four weeks to complete the selection procedure from initial nomination of candidates to final approval. And this process is continued in a cyclic manner in parallel to the Vocational Training for Gender Empowerment.

CONCLUSION

With implementing the Gender Empowerment scheme and harvesting favorable results in stipulated duration of time the BCCL Company has proven that ***existing legal loopholes*** can also be utilized as a platform for sustainable growth and development of the firm.

Because as as per rules of ***Directorate General of Mines Safety Act 46(b)*** women are not permitted to go into underground mines as well as per ***Mines Act 1952*** women are prohibited to enter the working mines after sunset and before sunrise. But with this Vocational Training Scheme the women can be permitted to work in operating mines in daytime before sunset and after sunrise to handle the heavy machineries.

The ***existing gap*** of day time working permit in functional mines, which was not utilized till date has been now adopted in a positive facet and has been exercised efficiently for progressive growth. For the first time this precedence has set an example of Gender Empowerment being practiced at ground level for optimum output for the Company.

Empowerment of feminine employees in the work place provides them with opportunities to make their own decisions with regards to their tasks. Gender empowerment among employees is one of the most important and emerging avenue in recent time. Companies ranging from small to large and from low-technology manufacturing concerns to high-tech software firms have been initiating gender empowerment programs to enhance employee motivation, increase efficiency, and gain competitive advantages in the turbulent contemporary business environment.

As merely by issuing free competitive forms, cheaper loans and concessions in higher education and railway journey tickets Gender Empowerment can't be done at a large scale. It is recommended that near about 50% reservations must be done in banking, health, education, judiciary and other office administration must be strictly done as soon as possible. As these are the arena which directly influences the decision making of National policies. This will accelerate the Gender Participation in policy making as well as in Decision Making process too.

This successful policy being flourishing after being formulated and implemented. It is strictly recommended that this case record must be made acquaint to maximum possible industries. So that more swift gender empowerment policies can be made and implemented too. Definitely this policy has uplifted the mark of intangible asset.

RECOMMENDATION

1) It is recommended that such gender empowerment policies must me more developed so as to enhance the Gender Empowerment. As well as this *"Paradigm of Blended Replica Model"* must be made acquaint to every Public Sector Undertaking company of India for inspiration to develop the avenues of gender Empowerment.

2) Among all the 250 Public Sector Undertaking Companies of Government of India, a healthy proportion of job opportunities must be sanctioned for women personnel in maximum permissible working portfolios. Especially among the post of Directors of these Public Sector Undertaking Companies of Government of India.

3) The rationale behind it is that all these Public Sector Undertaking Companies of Government of India are incorporated under Companies Act 1956, which advocates the mandatory provision of a minimum

of five (05) posts of Directors for the incorporation of the registered company.

4) It is advocated that a minimum of fifty percent of total posts on an aggregate scale of all the Public Sector Undertaking Companies has to be reserved for women. As the policy formulation and its implementation is done at tactical level of Pyramid, i.e. at the Board of Director Level. This will definitely empower women from top to bottom level with immediate effect. As well as at the higher official level there is no question of any problem of ***occupational safety hazards, professional hazardous*** of the profession during their work.

REFERENCES

1. Pahariya NC, Shrivastava Abhinav Kumar, Conference Paper Presentation, National Conference on Globalization and Women Empowerment, Titled "Social Impact on skill training in Education and it's leverage To Public Sector Undertaking Companies in India", Theme "Vocational Skills and Training to Empower Women in Public Sector Undertaking Companies in India Institute of Public Enterprises, Osmania University, Hyderabad held on 15-16th March 2012.

2. Shrivastava, Abhinav Kumar, Pahariya NC, Gender Empowerment in Practice: - A Case Study at BCCL, Dhanbad, International Journal of Research in Commerce, IT and Management, Volume No.(02),2012, Issue No.05 (May), ISSN 2231-5756.

3. Shrivastava AK, Workers' Participation in Management in Policy Making: - Roots and Routes for Prosperous Industrialized Economy, LAP Lambert Publication, Germany, ISBN: - 978-3-659-35799-2, Pp 65-80

CHAPTER#3

WPM Empowers Mutual Coordination and Occupational Safety

INTRODUCTION

The proposed case is a representation of a factual incident where a mutual support and healthy co-operation can be strongly identified between Management and Trade Unions. This real case is a chapter to expose the unfreezing and changing the attitude of both the Management as well as Trade Unions [1].

This real case study is structured and shaped taking the BCCL Katras (Bharat Cocking Coal Limited) Area into Account. The Katras Area is located at the central prime location of the BCCL (Bharat Coking Coal Limited) Company. The BCCL Company (Bharat Coking Coal Limited) is the world's largest Prime Coking Coal producing company as well as a NavRatna Company.

The BCCL Company is also the largest subsidiary in terms of manpower of the Maharatna Company "Coal India Limited". It provides the high calorific value coal for Bokaro steel industry in nearby and also for The Chandrapura thermal power plant.

This case study explains the caring and co-operative working style of both management and the representative of union to solve an industrial dispute. The paper has been drafted by interviewing the Union's representative as well as interviewing the victim labour of a serious accident, personally at his residence.

The result hence can be drawn the start of an era of ***win-win situation*** in Public Sector Undertakings and also in arena of Industrial Relations.

PRACTICAL REAL CASE STUDY

In a ground level case study it was found that it was a fog covered and extremely cold morning of January 10, 2010.The maximum of workmen were on rest as it was a pleasant Sunday. And the workmen whose Sunday duty was allotted were on the duty as it was a day of Inspection visit of the extreme high Powered regulatory authority for Mines Safety, the Directorate General of Mines Safety.

Parallel to this maximum key Executive, the representatives of major trade unions and the Safety experts were busy in collection and arranging the reports and suggestions to scrutinize the final draft to be presented at the desk of Safety Board to be held on January 21, 2010.

Breaking the peace suddenly an emergency siren blow up and then within fraction of a minute there was a huge uproar in the whole workplace of Katras Area. In a puzzled environment No one was able to answer anything except inferring that something unfortunate accident has happened.

No one was able to answer anything except inferring that something unfortunate accident has happened. From a peon to GM Chairperson Katras Area ran towards electric sub-station and found Mr. Laldhari Bhuian to be burnt badly with electric shock of 33000 Volts.Laldhari Bhuian has turned senseless but his body was shivering badly.

The accident was so deadly that the electric wire had inserted inside the body of Mr. Laldhari Bhuian and burnt his inner nerves and bones. Also the Body of Mr.Laldhari Bhuian was burnt badly from leg to head. The electric shock threw him about 30 feet far causing a deep injury to his head also. Mr. Bhuian was victim of "Electrocution Injury"

Soon Mr. Bhuian was carried to the primary health care centre and then to Bokaro Central Hospital and was placed in Intensive Care Unit. Everyone was asking continuous question to GM Chairperson Katras Area, related to safety and elimination of working hazards. But GM refused to tell anything without proper investigation.

Upon investigation it was initially found that due to heavy fog, Mr Laldhari Bhuian was unable to see a minor breakage in the wire connectivity of the transformer and also his foots slipped due to wet platform due to moist and at the end he cacthed wrong electricity junction with naked hand due to minor confusion.

These all situational factors lead to this disastrous accident. In corresponding to this the GM Chairperson, Katras Area, was keeping a regular watch for health of Mr Laldhari Bhuian.

It was January 18,2010, Mr Laldhari Bhuian's right hand was decided to be separated by surgery by the Doctors. After an operation of more than 6 hours the surgery was successful and finally he was certified to be out of danger by the Doctors. Meanwhile GM Chairperson, Katras Area, was asked a bunch of pressurized questions by media as well as from a few trade unions too. But he GM Chairperson, Katras Area, remained calm and silent in a decent manner, and didn't spoke a single word on the investigation report as per Company Protocols.

By next 72 hours the ***extremely high powered*** authority, Safety Board's meeting started on January 21,2010 and the single focus was to question GM Chairperson, Katras Area, on issues of safety responsibilities. After almost maximum person have charged GM for being non-vigilant on the safety issue.

At this extreme crucial time Mr. R.S. Tiwari who is Dy. General Secretary for Jharkhand State of AITUC and also the member of Safety board of the B.C.C.L. company; addressed the Public meeting by speaking that "The duty performed by our Respected GM Chairperson Katras Area is "respectable", "appreciable", "and an model example to be followed by all of us". (Please refer Figure 4).

Everyone turned stunned and all the members present in meeting turned attentive to hear Mr.Tiwari There was a pin drop silence in the meeting hall.

Mr. Tiwari continued "As Half truth is more dangerous than lie, for the same I am explaining the complete fact. I saw GM Chairperson running on the accident spot driving his duty jeep self, immediately he got the wireless message. And before the ambulance may arrive the workmen along with GM Chairperson escorted Shri.Laldhari Bhuian upto hospital. Always a ***first-aid*** box is always ready in all duty vehicles of BCCL Company."

At the same time many of our peer colleagues also came and driver took the steering to drive the car but I saw GM giving the initial first aid as ointments and pain-killer and also Mr Laldhari Bhuian was laying in unconscious stage in lap of GM while moving to the hospital, due to which life of Mr Laldhari Bhuian has been saved".

Mr Tiwari Continued "Due to strict implementation of the policy of the "*Safety Talk*" being exercised everyday by orders of GM Katras Area our family member Mr. Bhuian has been saved". Mr Tiwari added that "I found GM Chairperson, Katras Area, every morning and evening to meet the victim as well as consoling his family."

Mr. Tiwari added "It was January 18, 2010 when the surgery was to be done at Bokaro Hospital, he was GM Katras Area to be the first person to move to donate his blood to Mr Laldhari Bhuian. Every moment GM has cared the victim as a family member and as an elder brother."

Mr. Tiwari concluded "At the end I would like to say that due to active and empathetic attitude of GM the ***"Fatal Accident was changed to a serious*** *accident*". In my opinion such heroic rescue actions must be adopted as a role model to save the precious life of the workmen. Finally once again before I may stop let me re-articulate that the duty performed by our Respected GM is "respectable", "appreciable", "and a model example to be followed by all of us".

Figure 4. Mr. R.S.Tiwari, Dy. General Secretary,
AITUC, *State of Jharkhand, Republic of India.*

Everyone in Management as well as the representatives of the various Unions appreciated Mr.Tiwari and supported his statement in a single tone. And this action of statement of Mr. Tiwari started the chapter of co-operation and mutual trust in real life rather than to be discussed as a useless Hypothetical Theory.

And it has been for the *first time* in the page back history of mining industry that a "**Letter of Appreciation**" was awarded after the accident followed by rescue.

As in any mining industry the safety hazards as same as in the Coal mining Industry. The "**Letter of Appreciation**" was awarded to GM Chairperson, Katras Area by Honorable Chairman-Cum-Managing Director **Shri T.K.Lahiry** for the rescue and safety decisions made by GM even in toughest situations.

In addition to this it was instructed by Chairman-Cum-Managing Director of BCCL, Dhanbad, Shri T.K.Lahiry that every GM Chairperson of all the functional mines and departments must follow the working tactics for safety provisions from GM Katras Area to incorporate it in day to day working of the company.

In addition, the policy of "**Safety Talk**" also has been formulated and implemented by *Chairman-Cum-Managing Director of BCCL, Dhanbad Shri T.K.Lahiri.* In the "**Safety Talk**" Policy it was strictly instructed that every working personnel in mines must discuss and share their experience daily for duration of ten minutes. This was a platform to change the feedback.

In addition to this regularly the methods of first-aid and procedures of rescue was mandatorily to be discussed among workmen.

While on September 30th, 2011 Mr.Laldhari Bhuian was interviewed personally. It was found that his right hand burnt badly and left hand was removed from shoulder. Mr.Laldhari explained the complete episode in his own words. As It was wrong to ask much more to him as it may have hurt his sentiment. He told "I am safe due to my good deeds and blessings earned by the people. **Even if elephant sits idle then also he is tall than the horse in height.**"!!

Mr.Laldhari Bhuian can't eat food or even drink tea from his own hand. Also he use to take bath and use to change dress by help of his wife. And being very thankful to Management he expresses his thanks to the Management of BCCL Katras Area and he spoke "Management has taken my care as a parent of family".

Mr. Bhuian added "BCCL administration has given me Rs.300000 as a compensation for running the bread and butter of my 14 family members. Management has also taken care of my family while I was in Bokaro Hospital for more than six months continuously. And soon my Provident Fund's Money will be also granted to me. And as per laws after that my son will get job on behalf of my replacement"(Please refer Figure 5).

Mr. Bhuian turned emotional and a few drops of tears came out of his eyes. He spoke with a sheivering tone "Yeh Kushi ke aansu hain (These are tears of happiness). GM Saheb has send officials to get my signature on the official documents; I have not even moved a single inch for any of my official work. I am extremely thankful to Management. Also "GM Memsahab" (Spouse of GM Katras Area) has cared for women of my families as an elder sister by providing us all sort of help to us. I am blessed by BCCL Administration to receive outmost care at my doorsteps."

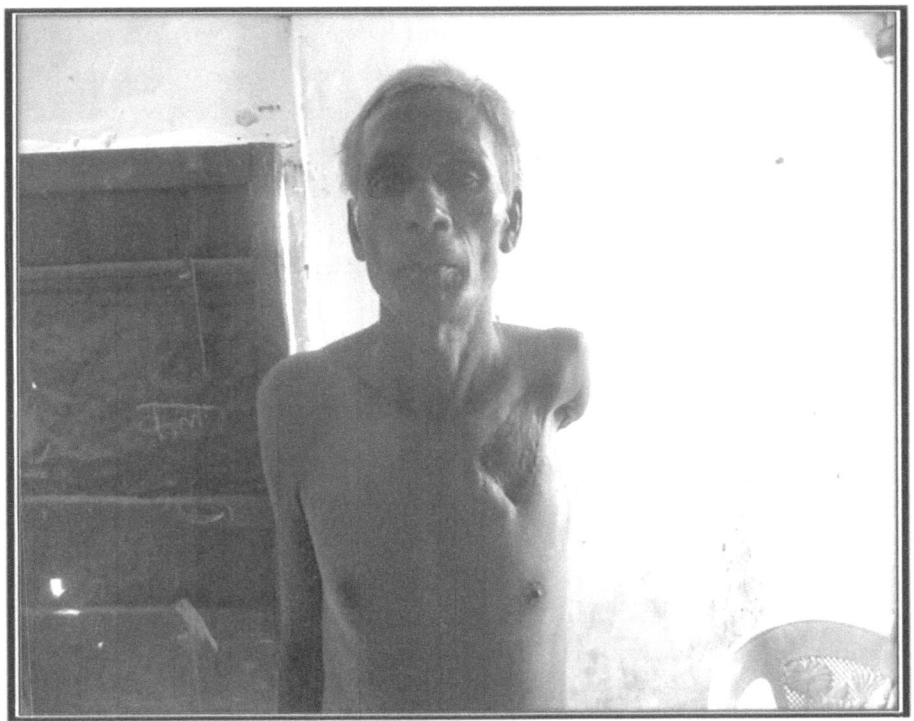

Figure 5. Mr. Laldhari Bhuian after the rescue.

This incident has gradually enhanced the knowledge level of workmen for professional safety as well as made them acquaint with the methods to combat disaster.

In addition to this on every weekend the workmen are also made aware with first aid treatment and other mock drills to handle the disasters and accidents.

Every day the minutes of meeting of the **"Safety Talk"** is being recorded and kept at desk of administrative authority. The policy is being exercised in every unit and clusters working in different locations of working mines.

This is also a precedence of **"Quality Circle"** and **"Decentralization"** in a healthy practice. The regular practice of **"Safety Talk"** has enriched the workmen even being formal literate to tackle the disaster and accident.

With a high morale Mr. Bhuian continued "I admit my mistake that even though everyone while discussion at **"Safety Talk"** every morning use to tell me about the importance of consciousness of safety, but I didn't took it ever seriously. As I was on verge of retirement so I was not serious. And all the colleagues working with me who sincerely and actively participated in the policy of **"Safety Talk"** every day are truly to be a tribute to save me from that worse circumstance. The policy of **"Safety Talk"** has given me a rebirth".

Mr. Bhuian added "This accident happened with me at age of 59.And if I would have retired and this accident would have happened later on then no one would have been able to take care of my 14 family members. In my religion a person is burnt after death in funeral and it is believed that his new birth as a human will occur. This accident has burnt me badly and also gave me a new birth."

Mr. Bhuian cleared his tears and continued "Now after my job's replacement to my son has made me free of worries and I can live happily with my family and grandchildren without any tension."

While interviewing on this brilliant rescue Mr Tiwari he told "At individual level I only see the positive aspects in every person and I work with an unbiased and co-operative attitude. Representatives of both the Management as well as of various unions have developed a wrong tendency to blame each other for personal gain and political mileage, but I oppose such intention and also I use to work with spirit of Brotherhood for welfare of all the people who trust me."

Mr. Tiwari continued "As safety policy is to curb occupational hazards, for the same I must support every working personnel who has pro-actively fulfilled their duties as our GM Chairperson has done. We can't lose a real follower of safety and rescue policies in a strict manner."

Mr. Tiwari also added that due to policy of **"Safety Talk"** once a few weeks back a major hydraulic fault was identified in Heavy vehicle which may not have damaged any life but the breakdown in the machinery would have definitely resulted into big financial loss and also would have slowed down the efficiency of working unit of the mines.

CONCLUSION

The case study done might seem like a narrated fictional pen sketch, but this episode has set a brilliant example of **healthy Industrial Democracy**. Both the Management and union have turned supportive towards each other. And as per author's opinion this has started the end of era of condemning each other.

Mr.Laladhari Bhuian has started a new phase of life. He can't even wear his dress and spectacles by himself. Nor he can walk speedily. He feels tired while he sits or speaks for more than half hour. He is having a non-stop echo sound in his ear.

But overcoming all this hurdles he use to teach ethical stories to the children of locality and makes daily prayer to God. He says "It is grace of God that I have been saved from 33000 Volt's shock, as with such a huge shock even steel would have melt down. Even **Rajdhani Express** run on 18000 Volts, I am thankful to God for new revival of my life".

Soon Mr. Laldhari Bhuian's son got the replacement job on his place with legal approval **Section 3 of Workmen Compensation Act 1923**. And it is well assured that his life will be not normal as before but definitely will be on right track.

Earlier Mr. Bhuian was a bit hesitate to speak but when it was requested that the interview is for academic purpose then He co-operated very gently while interview and also gave his photograph and video captions to the interviewer.

The author recommends the case of Mr. Bhuian must be endorsed to maximum of the intellectuals and industries as this will motivate both management and Unions to be co-operative for each other for welfare of the each other as well as the organization. (Please refer Figure 6). This case study motivates to conclude author's views that in any Industrial Organization the **Industrial Relation is the spine** of the industry. A minor fabrication to even the smallest tissue of this spine results into heavy damage. Mr. Bhuian's situation in this accident due to his own minor mistake was same as of an innocent victim on **"No-Man's Land"**; where the person have to face shoot outs from both the ends.

And the situation of Katras Area Management was same as of the individual who has been fake accused for any offence to the innocent who is under **non-bail able under trial** where the **innocent** can be saved only with statement of the victim.

And the Trade Union representative especially Mr. Tiwari has played a very important role to save the innocent under trial with substantiating the sequential incidents. Finally the B.C.C.L. administration has given an unbiased umbrella cover of protection to every person related to this case.

It was Mr.R.K.Tiwari's judgmental and rational statement on 21ˢᵗ January 2010 who ***stopped the administrative transfer*** on disciplinary ground and taint over character over GM Katras Area.

As Mr.Laldhari Bhuian was in hospital in a senseless stage for more than two months. And later the statement of Mr. Tiwari was also substantiated with sequel incidents that took place as well as with statements of Mr.Laldhari Bhuian too. Every individual in this case was innocent legally as well as morally.

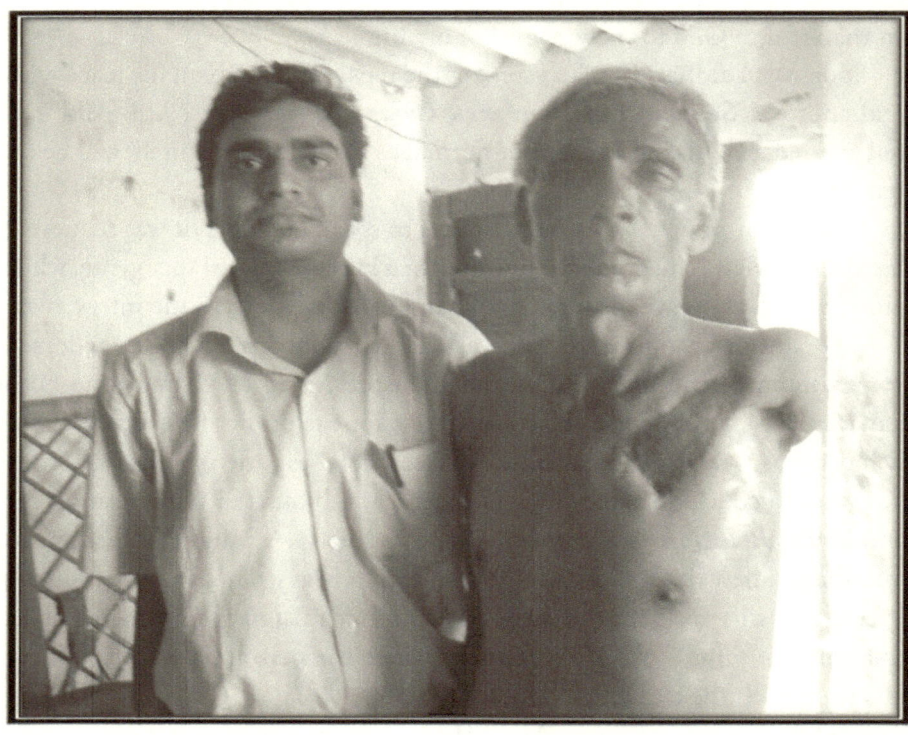

Figure 6. Author (Dr. Abhinav Kumar Shrivastava) with Mr. Laldhari Bhuian at Residence of Mr. Laldhari Bhuain after the interview.

Mr. Tiwari also concluded "If any action would have been taken on GM Katras Area, then this would have broken the mutual trust of management and union as well as a responsible leader as GM Katras Area would have being lost.

This episode has motivated both the worker as well as Management to work for a common welfares' goal with more enthusiasm and dedication. Furthermore a very strong trust has emerged among management, trade unions and labour force.

It is a well said prose that ***Justice hurried is justice buried and justice delayed is justice denied,*** it can be easily concluded that with proper cooperation and mutual Industrial Harmony a swift expansion can be done in any Industry for growth and development.

This real case study has also proven the sustainability in terms of ***"Industrial Sustainability"*** as due to any dispute if the working of any organization stops even for a day or even due to half hearted attitude of workmen the production declines then it makes a loss of billions on an overall national scale. Such precedence further motivates the workmen and management to work safely with precautionary measures as well as to make healthy cooperation mutually.

REFERENCES

1. Pahariya NC, Shrivastava Abhinav Kumar, Paper Presented titled "Escalation of Unfreezing Attitude of Workmen Representative and Management, National Seminar on Best Practices in HR For Sustainability, Theme:- IR, Labor Laws and Sustainability, Conference Proceedings vide *ISBN Number 9788184247541*, Institute of Public Enterprises, Osmania University, Hyderabad dated 23rth-24rth February 2012.

2. Shrivastava AK, Workers' Participation in Management in Policy Making: - Roots and Routes for Prosperous Industrialized Economy, LAP Lambert Publication, Germany, ISBN: - 978-3-659-35799-2, Pp 81-95.

CHAPTER#4

WPM in Elimination of Sexual Harassment Grievances

INTRODUCTION

The term Gender Empowerment in actual sense is coined for protection for both the genders, i.e. to make **equilibrium** between both **feminine and masculine gender**, especially at Professional workplace. But generally the term gender empowerment is ***misunderstood as "Only Women Empowerment".*** As *half truth* is more dangerous than lie, hence misinterpretation of knowledge is also very dangerous. The proposed paper elaborated the comparative contrast study of two innocent people being harmed by non-use and misuse of the legal powers. The Gender empowerment can only be done when the law is enforced with neutral, committed and unbiased attitude. The discussed two cases elaborate the *legal loopholes* which are to be filled up[1].

As India is the largest human manpower, and hence if a unique Policy of designed for every personnel of all the industries. And definitely it will result as a precedence of Empowerment all around the globe. As well as a main segment of "***Workers' Participation in Management in Policy Making***" there will be tremendous job opportunities in coming era of Industrialized Economy"

Honorable Supreme Court of India gave strict ruling "It is duty of the employer to prevent or deter the committing of any act of sexual harassment at the work place". For the same this case study will be a precedence to all employers as well as Government agencies that the well acquaintance with the rulings of Honorable Supreme Court of India of *"Sexual Harassment at workplace"* must be made mandatory part of Induction schedule to every new employee who joins the organization.

The same will enhance the efficiency of women personnel with assurance of proctored environment as well as the awareness among men and women personnel with increase by uplifting of **"Decent Professional Expertise"** in Work Culture. The same will result into Ethical protection to emerging sustainable paradigms in Business, Entrepreneurship, Law of Land and all facets of employment. As balanced and proctored environment at work place can only assure the sustainable development of organization.

OBJECTIVES

1) To make intellectuals aware of **"non-use"** and **"misuse"** of the Constitutional rights and provisions of legal powers enacted.
2) To acquaint intellectuals the power of **"Legal Knowledge"** to implement accurately at required time.

METHODOLOGY

The methodology involves the personal interview as a part of absolute primary source of data collection. As well as the Online news as well as videos from social networking are taken as secondary form of data. The **positive shades** of these two comparative case studies are highlighted by **bold fonts** and ***bold italics fonts*** for better understanding of the readers.

LITERATURE REVIEW

Ruling of Honorable Supreme Court of India in the Vishaka and others V. State of Rajasthan and others, (AIR 1997 SUPREME COURT 3011) J.S. Verma C.J.I., Mrs. Sujata V. Manohar and B.N. Kirpal. JJ, has been taken into account for framing the real case study.

CASE STUDY

The proposed two case studies elaborate two different comparative real case studies of the extreme atrocity against two innocent people. The first case is of a lady **I.A.S. Officer (Indian Administrative Services Officer),** Dr. Madhurani Teowtia, whose husband Late Shri. Narendar Singh was a gallant and extreme honest I.P.S. officer (Indian Police Services Officer). Late Narendar Singh and was brutally murdered while combing with organized mining mafia.

Unfortunately this heinous accident happened on ***08th March, 2012*** which is celebrated as ***International Women's day*** as well as it was the ***scared colorful Indian festival of "Holi" of Hindu Religion on that date.*** The lady I.A.S. officer was in ninth month pregnancy at the time she lost her brave husband. In the pregnancy stage she herself as a brave lady did funeral of her husband.

The lady I.A.S. officer could have easily got justice under protective ruling of Honorable Supreme Court of India with reference of ***Vishakaha v/s state of Rajasthan*** by arresting and severe punishment for guilt and conspirators.

CASE

The case is of for Lady I.A.S. Officer Dr. Madhurani Teowtia, an I.A.S. Officer of 2008 Batch at Madhya Pradesh Cadre. She was awarded the best probationer award in her batch in Madhya Pradesh Cadre for her excellent administrative performance during rigor training as an I.A.S probationer. Her Husband Late Shri Narendra Singh, was a brave I.P.S. officer who was posted in risky area of *"Stone Mining Mafia"*.

As an honest officer Late Shri Narendra Singh, made more than dozen of raids in just 45 days from his posting and cancelled many licenses too for the transportation activity in the Morena District of Madhya Pradesh. On March 08th,2012 Late Shri Narendra Singh was on police patrolling with his team and he tried to stop a tractor carrying illegal mined stones. He was brutally crushed by the tractor. Later his wife Dr. Madhurani Teowatia did his funeral in stage of pregnancy of ninth month. After funeral of Late Shri Narendra Singh, his family demanded for CBI probe for extending the enquiry. March 08th is **"International Women's Day"** as well as it was the festival of colors **"Holi"** that date of Calendar Year.

On demand of CBI inquiry, the response of political kingpins was heinous and horrible. One of the political leaders; Shree Kailash Vijayvargiya Jee spoke in front of media *Jo hoga hum dekh lenge, humne chooriya nahi pehan rakhi hain (We will handle what it may be, we have not worn bangles)*. And on this statement the whole system kept silence and no legal or administrative action has been still taken against Shree Kailash Vijayvargiye.

Father of Late Shri Narendra Singh cried and Spoke "Our son's sacrifice is nothing more than "death of dog" in eyes of politicians. Still we get threatening calls from Government that we will be more tortured. If my Daughter-in-law was awarded best I.A.S. probationer then why she was transferred? When politician want to get a groom they want I.A.S. or I.P.S., but now they question the supreme sacrifice of my son?"

He added **"Duniya ka sabse bada dukh ek baap ke liye hai jawan eklautey bete ka jana, par uss se zyada mujhe khushi hai ek imaandar** aur saheed sipahi ka baap hona (The most painful punishment for a father is to see his only young and dynamic son dead but more than this I have happiness to be known as father of a honest martyr solider)"

In a Public interview the acting Superintendent of Archeological Survey of India, Shri K.K. Muhaamad expressed his pain of dominating mining Mafia. On Evening of March 08th, 2012 **Shri K.K.Muhaamad** spoke to media in an interview that "*Stone and mining Mafia* are very powerful. They are even many times more powerful than dacoits of Chambal Region". It was found that as a **"Decent and Ethical Muslim"** Shri K.K. Muhammad was dedicatedly working in reconstruction of a **sacred Hindu Temple** in the Morena and Chambal region. The vibrations due to illegal mining Mafia was creating problem for structure of Temple. Shri K.K.Muhammad wrote to Superintendent of Police, District Collector, and District Forest Officer. But no action was taken against illegal mining Mafia.

Due to high vibrations from blasting and mining the Temple would have been collapsed. Shri K.K. Muhaamad turned very much worried to **save the sacred Hindu Temple.** In a stressed situation Shri K.K. Muhaamad wrote a letter to then acting Chief of RSS (Rastriya Swayam Sevak Sangh) Shri Sudarashan Jee Maharaj.

Shri Sudarshan Jee Maharaj took the issue as a **guardian** and as a **"Decent and Ethical Hindu"** he exercised his caring **Parental attitude** to help Shri K.K.Muhammad Sir. It was Shri Sudarshan Jee Maharaj's tall social image that that problem of illegal mining was stopped immediately with his ethical interference in the subject.

Now a question arises that do such neat and ethical leadership as of Shree Sudarshan Jee Maharaj is not required at every step to curb corruption and eliminate crime and Organized Mafia? Especially when it is **issue of Protection and Honor of a Women**, may or may not be an I.A.S officer. As well as **protection of life of an innocent and brave person** may be or may not be and I.P.S. Officer!!

This topic has still to be discussed and a strong policy must be executed as soon as possible to **protect honor of all Woman with supreme priority** with assurance of security of life of every common man.

Dr Madhurani Teowtia shared her pain and spoke to media "I have believe in **I.A.S. and I.P.S** as these are **constitutional institutions**, but I feel pain to say that I don't have faith in the personnel involved in it. The tractor driver who crushed my husband is a tool to stop the right and punishment must be made to hands handling these tools. I have pardoned the tractor driver as he is just a puppet. But I feel extreme pain to say that the combing against corruption started by my brave husband is brutally crushed, but this sacrifice of my martyr husband has started a new chapter of combat against corruption".

FINDINGS

1) The provisions laid by Honorable Supreme Court of India have either been not "**Enforced accurately**" or is being used as a "***Cyanide Element***" to terminate the innocent.

2) The laws for civil protection are to be properly nurtured from grassroots level seed to a grown up mature fruit bearing tree rather than to implant and graft the various branches for instantaneous "***Unethical benefit and personal gains***".

3) The very Famous Proverb "**Justice Hurried is Justice Buried and Justice Delayed is justice denied**" turns true in situations where the victim of injustice as well as innocent facing the conspiracy charges are not acquaint with legal shield provided to them.

4) Even though many times when awareness is with the victim, the victims don't know the pathway channel to legal aid. In these cases the ***non-awareness of legal pathway*** as well as the **simple access to legal pathway** both has been elaborated.

CONCLUSION

From the CASE it is easily concluded that strict disciplinary action would have been taken against Mr. Kailash Vijay Vargiye for his uncivilized speech for family of Late Shri Narendra Singh. Either he should have kept absolute silence on issue or at least he must have spoken some supportive words. As per IPC 509, **even a single word or gesture which outrage modesty of women or directly or indirectly creates annoyance or unethical word must be treated as a serious crime.**

Shree Kailash Vijayvargiye has earned lots of accolades for social and civilian developments by his political service. His efforts are commendable in bringing the I.I.Ts and I.I.Ms in state of Madhya Pradesh. He is also known as a good strategist in politics. So an indecent speech from him is not expected. At least the complete Administration must have created pressure on Shree Kailash VijayVargiya, so as to ask ***Humble apologize*** and to make a public declaration of ***taking his word back with promise of non repentance of such uncivilized action***.

FUTURE SCOPE

In Future all around the globe the lot of job opportunities will be welcoming Women Professionals in working Industry. The awareness of empowerment dictum guided by Law of Land will enable the swift Gender Empowerment as well as a culture of mutual respect and coordination will enhance the trustworthiness and intangible value of organizations.

ADMINISTRATIVE RESTRUCTURING

1) In every district, either the post of Superintendent of Police or District Magistrate must be reserved for Women.
2) In every state, either the post of Director General of Police or Chief Secretary of State must be reserved for Women.
3) These basic administrative restructuring will have a very high impact on measures of "Gender Empowerment" in a swift manner.

LIMITATIONS

1) The present limitations of Gender Empowerment are the mindset of common people especially in India who are ***biased with thinking of Gender discrimination.***
2) As well as the top chair and the policy makers including democratic representatives are not pro-active for unbiased Gender Empowerment.
3) The ***socio-political custodianship*** must be adopted for ***unbiased, neutral and committed Gender Empowerment.***

RECOMMENDATIONS

1) If we can create social networking accounts then we must also create our account at door steps of web domain of Honorable Supreme Court of India.
2) We all must start a new environment of work with mutual respect for every person.
3) We must not disturb the Honorable Judiciary on minor issues as well as the accessibility to the Honorable Judiciary must not be used as a *"Lottery Bag"*. There must be a sense of ethical respect towards every person who is working together in a joint office environment.

REFERENCES

1. Shrivastava, Abhinav Kumar, "Gender Empowerment at Professional Workplace, Conference Paper Presentation"; "National Conference on Paradigm for Sustainable Business: - People, Planet and Profit", Department of Management Studies, Indian Institute of Technology, Roorkee during 08-09 March, 2013.

2. Original thoughts of Dr. Abhinav Kumar Shrivastava, A Common Honest and Ethical Indian, Unique Identity: - Indian Passport Identity number "H 9 7 9 5 1 1 4".

3. Shrivastava AK, Workers' Participation in Management in Policy Making: - Roots and Routes for Prosperous Industrialized Economy, LAP Lambert Publication, Germany, ISBN: - 978-3-659-35799-2, Pp 96-128.

CHAPTER#5

Relevance of WPM at International Stage

INTRODUCTION

While expanding the jurisdiction of importance of **_Workers' Participation In Management in Policy Making_** at global stage, the precedence of Kansai International Airport (KIA) accelerate the uprising significance of workers' involvement in feedbacks and decision making as a global precedence of success of concept of Workers' Participation in Management[1].

REAL CASE STUDY

The KIA open 24 hours per day, unlike its predecessor in the city. The *KIA* operates 614 international passenger flights, 200 international freighter flights and about 495 domestic passenger and freighter flights every week. Kansai International Airport is connected only by the Sky Gate Bridge R, a road cum Railroad Bridge to Rinku Town and the mainland [3].

The lower railroad level of the bridge is used by two railroad operators:-

(1) West Japan Railway JR West.
(2) Nankai Electric Railway.

The JR West operates Haruka, the limited express train services for Kansai Airport Station from Tennoji, Shin-Ōsaka and Kyoto Station.

JR West also offers "Kansai Airport Rapid" services for Kansai Airport Station from Osaka and Kyobashi Station, as well as several stations on the way. (Please refer Figure 7).

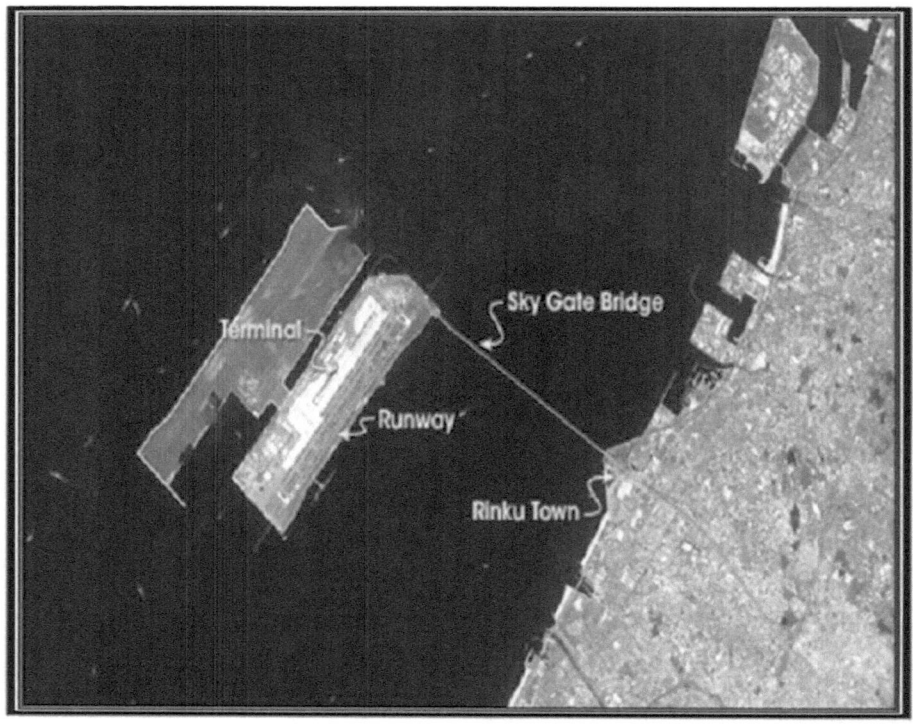

Figure 7. A Bird's Eye View of Kansai International Airport.

In the 1960s, when the Kansai region was rapidly losing trade to Tokyo, planners proposed a new airport near Kobe and Osaka. Osaka International Airport, located in the densely populated suburbs of Itami and Toyonaka, was surrounded by buildings; it could not be expanded, and many of its neighbors had filed complaints because of noise pollution problems.

After the protests surrounding New Tokyo International Airport now Narita International Airport, which was built with expropriated land in a rural part of Chiba Prefecture, planners decided to build the airport offshore.

The new airport was part of a number of new developments to revitalize Osaka, which had lost economic and cultural ground to Tokyo for most of the century. Initially, the airport was planned to be built near Kobe, but the city of Kobe refused the plan, so the airport was moved to a more southerly location on Osaka Bay. There, it could be open 24 hours per day, unlike its predecessor in the city.

The KIA operates 614 international passenger flights, 200 international freighter flights and about 495 domestic passenger and freighter flights every week. Kansai International Airport is connected only by the Sky Gate Bridge R, a road cum Railroad Bridge to Rinku Town and the mainland. The lower railroad level of the bridge is used by two railroad operators, The West Japan Railway JR West and Nankai Electric Railway. JR West operates Haruka, the limited express train services for Kansai Airport Station from Tennoji, Shin-Ōsaka and Kyoto Station. JR West also offers "Kansai Airport Rapid" services for Kansai Airport Station from Osaka and Kyobashi Station, as well as several stations on the way.

Various connections, such as buses, subways, trams, and other railroads, are available at each station. Nankai operates **RAPIT**, a limited express train service to Namba Station on the southern edge of downtown Osaka. Subway connections are available at Namba and Tengachaya Station. In July 2007 a high-speed ferry service run by Kaijo Access Co. began operating between Kobe Airport and KIX. The journey takes about thirty minutes.

The Main Terminal building of Kansai International Airport KIX is one of the most appealing structures of its kind, not just in Japan, but anywhere in the world. The four-story structure is a 1.7 kilometer-long aluminum and glass frame topped off with a roof which arcs in the shape of an undulating wing. It is World's first international airport made floating on sea with a 3,500 meter runway.

The sea wall is made of Rocks and 48,000 tetrahedral concrete blocks. The excavation was done for filling about 21 million cubic meters which is equivalent to 3 mountains. A 30 meter of layer of soil was implanted over sea floor and inside sea wall. A total of 1 billion dollar was spent for developing the connection bridge.

The initial sinking estimation was about 19-25 feet in next 50 years, but it sank about 8 metres 24 feets approx within two years of its active operation. The main reason found for speedily sinking of *KIA* was the "enormous jerk" of air vehicles while landing over the airport. These continuous jerks made the clay and soil in basement of the airport loose and which gradually mixed up with water. This resulted in speedily sinking of the airport.

The pumping system was installed to evacuate the additional water penetrating the basement of the airport. It was found that the Alluvial Soil gets liquefies when shaken due to jerks of the landing aircrafts. As well as the bottom layer of clay use to get damped due to excessive pressure.

This gradually led the *KIA* to sink at a very fast rate. This resulted into a thunder disaster situation for the Engineers and authorities. The administration of *KIA* exercised the theory of ***"Quality Circle"*** into practice by creating small teams of 5-8 workmen and assign task to find the causes and solutions for the problem of sinking of "*KIA*".

The reason found was the enormous jerk of aircraft landing. But the situation was turning tenser every moment due to lack of feasible solution. The feedback of workmen suggested that the hydraulic cylinders and pillars must be supported from base to stop sinking of "*KIA*". As it would be cost effective with less time to implement as well as the problem to work under the water will be solved. Soon as the suggestion was given it was scanned and filtered by the Expert Engineers and the full scale plan was ready.

In order to absorb the jerk created by landing of flights causing sink of *KIA*, a special hydraulic cylinder was made and installed, with an ordinary length usually calculated. As well as the bottom of these hydraulic cylinders were made in a manner so that they may be filled and supported with metallic plates.

This was done in order to fill the gap caused annually in order to make the *KIA* safe from sinking, which occurs due to heavy jerks created by landing of airplanes.

As a parallel action the water pumps were also installed to take out the water if the water may penetrate the bottom layer and may create the situation of "Under water flood" (Please refer Figure 8). And now annually the *KIA* is having replacement of bottom level of hydraulic cylinder installed as per the level of sinking.

The investment cost in maintenance of *KIA* is negligible cost as it raises a nominal cost of metallic plates being welded and installed with a labour cost of 15-20 working days.

This dream project would have sunk down resulting into a gigantic financial loss as well as a major blockade in the Japanese Economy. It was a real exercise of the concept of ***"Workers' Participation in Management in Policy making"*** for re-establishing of a gigantic Organization.

With Synergy of Labor skill, after the successful implementation of concept of refilling the base support of hydraulic supports it was made a mandatory policy to increase the frequency of feedback of workmen for all possible suggestion for development, sustainable growth, scope for expansion of the infrastructure of *KIA* as well as all possible risk to be identified at initial level, so that the risk can be mitigated in nascent stage only (Please refer Figure 9).

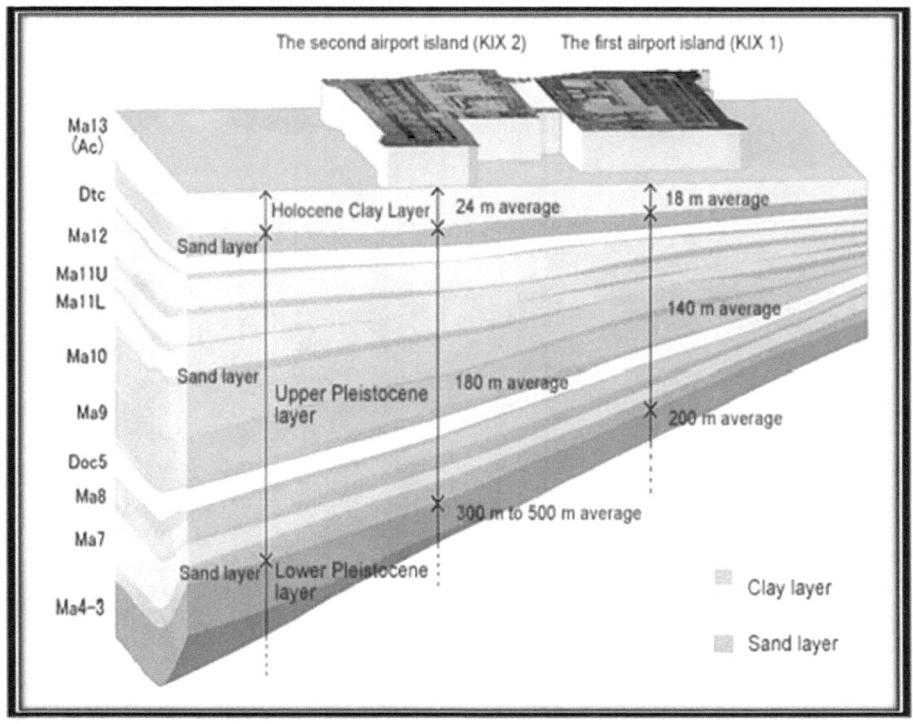

Figure 8. A view of bottom structure developed for making of the Kansai International Airport.

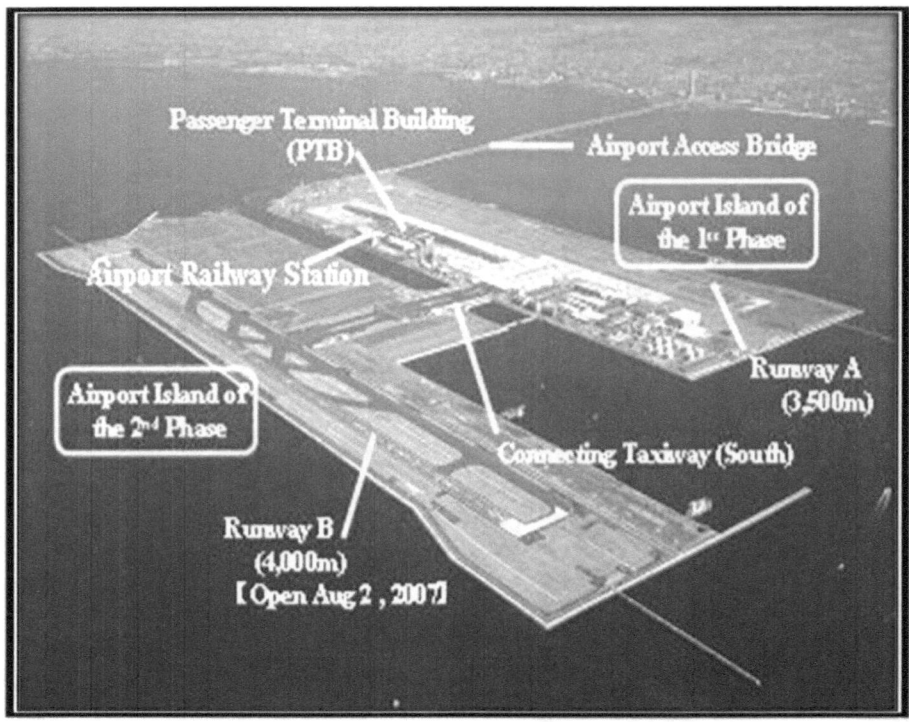

Figure 9. The Arial View of both the Airport Islands of Kansai International Airport.

The precedence of case of enduring smooth operational status of "Kansai International Airport" has set up a milestone for ***"Gainful utilization of Workmen's feedback and experience"***. This case study has set up a benchmark of absolute coordination of workmen and Management's approach to collect Human Factor in Innovation.

In a ***"Sea-Locked"*** island country like Japan the air connectivity is only the respiration option to the economy. With increasing global connectivity of flights the *KIA* has provided an expanded platform to boot up the National Economy. Possibly for the first time it may have occurred that an investment in Infrastructure would have such a nominal maintenance cost. Further there was an absolute ***"Zero Rehabilitation"*** cost occurred in making of KIA.

The core sector Industries are the spine of any nation. And all industries have flourished and also have expanded globally due to swift connectivity of Japan to whole globe through *KIA*. Role of workmen has a historical record of their importance in all the infrastructures constructed. But possibly the mitigation of sinking of *KIA* may be the first active operational infrastructure which have been secured by eradicating the huge problem by help of feedback and suggestions of Workmen. Further it was experience of workmen which made the installation of hydraulic pillars and their maintenance annually (Please refer Diagram 3).

The workmen also help in a channelized manner for making the *KIA* from huge debt over it as well as to achieve its targeted financial profit. The *KIA* has resulted the aviation connectivity of Japan in broader spectrum from rest countries of world. Now *KIA* is free from any danger of sinking till 2035.

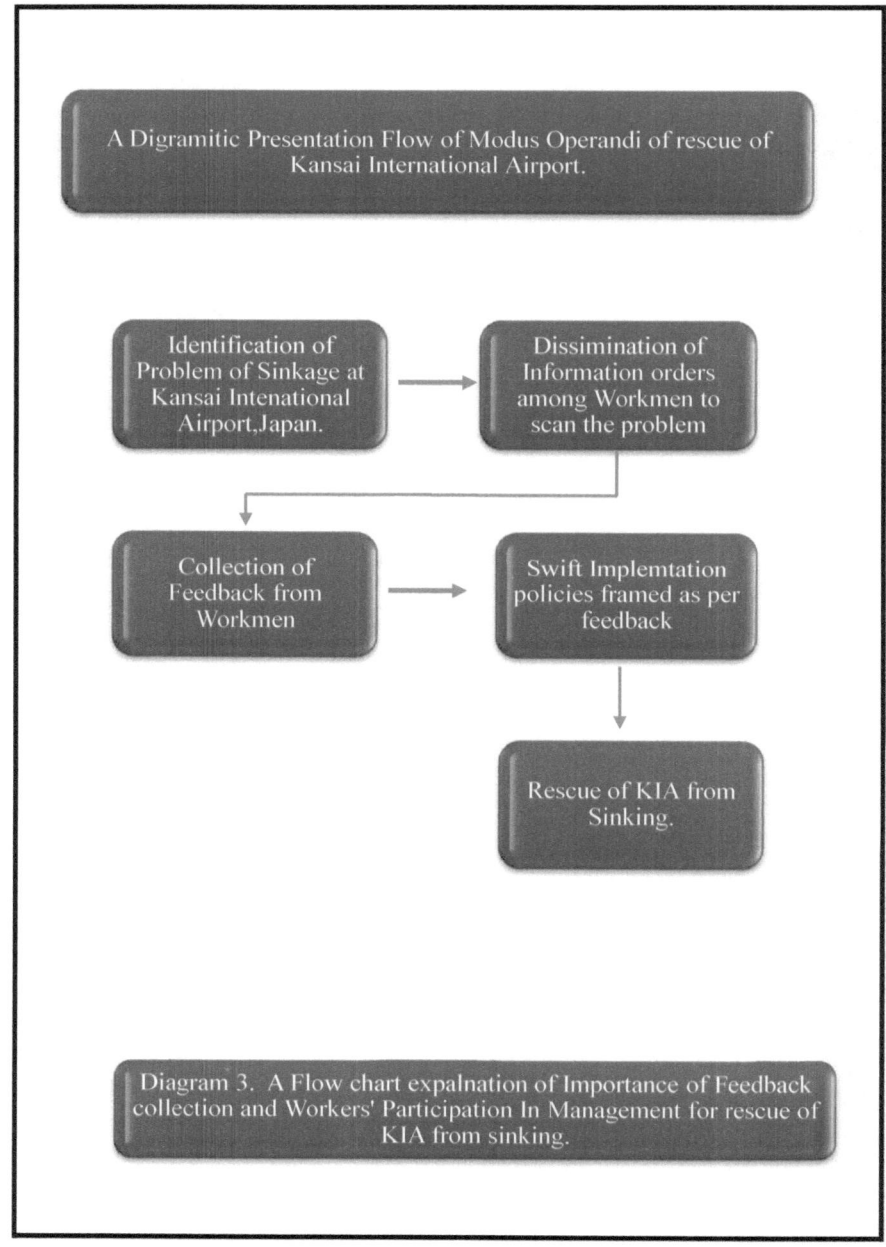

CONCLUSION AND RECOMMENDATION

As well as proposals is that till 2035, after the investment cost reimbursed with achieving the Break-Even status; from financial profit earned from *KIA* *a* new, much bigger than *KIA* and more advance airport will be developed from the profit earned. The role of workmen has an impact of ***"Thresh-hold Energy Point"*** which changes the results completely in minute fraction of time with a very little effort.

In developmental status of Workers' Participation in Management (WPM), now it is a healthy environment when the workers' participation in management must switch in making of policy framing and also in exercise of decision making. The paradigm of WPM must shift into permanent phase of ***"Workers' Participation in Management in Policy Making."***

A global record database must be maintained where the experience of Workmen must be recorded and compiled biannually so that the problem solving techniques must get boost up by exchange and share of ideas, experience and manual techniques.

The experience recorded of workmen must be audited by technical experts and experts of the related field so as to draft the knowledge in a well compiled manner for easy access of information. The experience database must be accessible in maximum possible language all over the world.

Movies of short duration ranging from 30 minutes to 45 minutes must be displayed of various problems being mitigated by virtue of help and feedback of workmen. This will motivate the workmen to work more dedicatedly as well as it will also inspire the workmen to share their experience about their work.

REFERENCES

1. Pahariya NC, Shrivastava Abhinav Kumar, Kansai International Airport: - An Incandescent Paradigm of Exercise of Workers' Participation In Management In Policy Making, IJMRS's International Journal of Management Sciences, Vol. 01, Issue 04, December 2012, ISSN: 2277-968X.
2. Shrivastava AK, Workers' Participation in Management in Policy Making: - Roots and Routes for Prosperous Industrialized Economy, LAP Lambert Publication, Germany, ISBN: - 978-3-659-35799-2, Pp 129-139.
3. http://en.wikipedia.org/wiki/Kansai_International_Airport

CHAPTER#6

Significance of WPM in Cadre Coordination

The Harmonic rhythm flow of workmen result into best output. A visit was made to open cast coal mines of Northern Coal Fields Limited. The working mines of Northern Coalfields Limited, Singrauli was started in year 1977 with an aim to satisfy the increasing the demand of energy of India. It is one of the nine sister subsidiaries of Coal India Limited Company. (Please See Figure 10)

In mid 1970s the major machineries and technologies were procured by both the superpowers of the time, the USA and erstwhile USSR. Having a long life with warranty the both superpowers contributed the major machineries to activate the working of the mines. And this process continued with expansion of gauge to procure more sophisticated machineries and technologies from various other countries too as Germany, United Kingdom, France, Japan etc. All these machineries have different parameters for handling them. These parameters are "**Very similar**" but not "**Exactly Same**". But with developing of "Common Parameter" to handle all the machineries and proper training at "Vocational Training Centers" the workmen have been made competent enough to handle the same machineries of different origin as well as different machineries of same origin nation too.

This has made the NCL Company as one of the largest profit making companies among public sector undertakings as well as of CIL subsidiary too. The mechanism of cadre coordination has initiated a new modus operandi to work with absolute safety and brilliant "Technological synchronization" even in the toughest working situations by the workmen.

Figure 10. An opencast mines of Jayant Project, NCL Singrauli, M.P.

The Northern Coalfields Limited [N.C.L.] Company is one of the subsidiaries of the Coal India Limited Company. The uniqueness of the N.C.L. Company is that it is a conjunction of mines which is having all the 100% working mines as opencast mines.

In addition to this the mines are designed to be fully mechanized mines. The working mines of NCL Singrauli is being operated with coordination of many departments cadre together as Mining for mining duty, Excavation Handling of Machineries, Electrical & Mechanical for maintenance of all machineries of mines, Telecommunication for handling communication devices used in mines, Materials Management Inventory Stockpile, Sales-Control and Planning for E-Auction, Merry-Go-Round Railway for coal transportation to nearest thermal power plant.

The mines are being operated for production resulting into financial profit with brilliant coordination of workmen of the company. The major work as told by experts in working mines is to excavate out the coal for processing.

And it is done by help of operating heavy mining machineries and blasting of explosives every day to remove the overburden and to excavate out the coal with proper coordination.

The *"Material Monetary Resources"* are the key factors for smoothly operating any working mines. Either the mines are for coal excavation or for any other mineral production, the basic methodology and the machineries are almost common in use.

The "Safety Audit" is one of the most essential factors for "Zero Accident Zone" and that can be only achieved with regular exercise of the safety provisions with perfect training being imparted. The various specialized cadres are working together with different machineries together at a time for overall production. These cadres are performing smooth due to promptness and perfection in working of the workmen.

The major of the personnel engaged in the operating mining activities are workmen only from different cadres.

The Shovel machines in the visited area were coded differently in numbers as "B-7" and "B-0" (See Figure 6). The experts made acquaint that the shovel "B-7" is a Russian model [USSR model] procured in early 1982 while the "B-0" is a Japanese model being procured in mid 1990s. The "Dragline" machine which is being handled by workmen only is a British model of machinery.

Similarly the overburden transporting "Dumpers" are from USA, Australia, United Kingdom Great Britain (See Figure 7). And finally many of the "Shovel" Machines which are engaged to load and off load the coal are manufactured by Japanese Technology.

It is the well grooming policies of the training imparted by "Vocational Training Centre" that the workmen are competent enough to handle the different machineries for same work as well as for different work at the same time with best mutual "Cadre-Coordination". As found that the world's third largest mechanical machine "Dragline", the heavy "Non-Road Moving Vehicles" as "Dumpers", the implantation of explosives by modern technology of "Sight Mixed Slurry" are being operated by trained workmen by help of the Drilling Machines (See Figure 11).

The workmen have well amalgamated the different parameters of machineries to a "Common Scale Parameter" to perform smoothly. These developed "Common Scale Parameter" to operate the machineries are "not exactly same" but "extremely similar" to each other for smooth and harmonic performance of the machineries in working mines.

Figure 11. Shovel Machineries at opencast mines at NCL Jayant Project.

1 = Workmen, 2 = Russian Model Shovel Machinery, 3= USA model machinery, 4= Workmen handling the machinery with coordination.

Figure 12. The Front and Rear View of Dumpers being
used for Excavated soil and excavated coal transportation at
NCL Jayant Project, Singrauli, Madhya Pradesh
(These "Non-Road Moving Vehicles are being operated by workmen")

Figure 13. The drilling Machine at NCL Jayant
Project, Singrauli, Madhya Pradesh.
These "Super – Sophisticated" machineries are being operated by workmen.

The working mines of Singrauli area are first fully mechanized opencast coal mines of India. These mines are the prime source of raw material provider in form of coal to National Thermal Power Corporation to produce electricity and satisfy the demanding energy needs of country.

These mines have many heavy machineries and mining technologies being implemented from many other countries. And it is a matter of appraisal that the workmen are being able to handle these all machineries all together all around the clock throughout the year with a brilliant coordination of handling the various machineries and technology together.

The project is a functional productive unit of the Northern Coalfields Limited, Dist of Singrauli in Madhya Pradesh. The Jayant Project is one of the largest working mines in terms of the Coal Production in India. The mines of N.C.L. Singrauli are one of the oldest open-cast working mines in India. The visit to operational blasting site was approved to be visited by Administrative Authorities at West Section of the working mines of Jayant Project.

While it was about one hour left in hand, the call was made by the experts and the senior administrative authorities to report to the West Section. While moving towards the working mines which is located about 20 kilometers from the residential colonies, it was found that a lot of greenery has been implanted as an environmental care measure in the route to the mines. The design of colonies and their maintenance is done *"Civil Department Cadre"*.

By moving ahead the mobility of traffic movement suddenly reduced as the restricted and the hypersensitive zone has started. The zone is the pathway to move to the functional working mines and only the permitted vehicles are allowed to move inside.

In parallel to the active road there is a starting separate road starts for movement of only heavy machineries. In these separate roads for the machineries the small vehicles are not permitted to move in. The cloud due to dust in atmosphere affects eye and respiration.

The cloud has emerged from the functional working mines and the coal being excavated out. In the pathway the "Regional Store" of the working was found. It was told by the guiding experts that the complete inventory management and the stockpile needs of the running and working mines are being preserved in the Regional Store so that the required items can be supplied to the working site.

This concept in practice is exercised to make a "Zero Delay" supply of all mining items to the demanded working site. Further the items required in mines are being kept in store in ample amount to avoid any shortage. The "Regional Store" is operated by the *"Materials Management Department Cadre"*. While moving ahead it was found that the giant size working mines was divided into two sections, the East Section and the West Section. Both the sections are being handled to excavate out the soil and the coal chunk is being harvested from between both working sections.

The coal is being received from the working unit named the "Central Pit". After crossing the final security post the final move was made to the working mines site. It was noticed that a lot of spare parts in form of scraps were kept unused. The security gadgets as helmet and shoes are being finally checked at the final entry port of mines. The safety gadgets as helmet and shoes must be even to be wear inside the moving closed vehicle to avoid any form of risk. So this is a positive sign of WPM that strict security measures are being followed.

The final start of absolute barren roads started. This barren roadway is found to be over burdened by soil, but these soiled roads were well pitched. As told by the experts that boundaries are being pitched for safety reasons from both the sides of the road. Further boundaries were also wired with strong and heavy metallic wires.

While moving ahead it was found that a huge machinery named as "Girder" was moving continuously for leveling and making the roadways to mines smooth. This is a continuous and all around clock job so as to make a smooth connectivity to the mines from the residential area. As due to the heavy quarry continuous all around the clock the roads get damaged and dumped also at many places.

It has been identified by Geology and Mineral experts with identification of many new coal patches. These coal blocks have been allocated to be operated nationwide to satisfy the growing demand of energy. At this junction a lot of machineries and sophisticated technologies are to be procured in future in the operating mines. These technologies are being procured from different countries as well as different firms of the same countries too. While the technology is procured from different countries then the "Handling Procedure" of the machineries is different for the same work, as well as the situation is almost same for the same machineries manufactured from different firm of a same country.

For example the heavy transportation machineries from USA works with left hand drive as well as on measures of electricity is in "Volts". While on other hand the machineries being procured from erstwhile USSR Union of Soviet Socialistic Republic have the right hand drive and have the measures of electricity transformation in "Watts" and in few models in "Ampere" too. Similarly in modern context to start up new operating mines the most modern mining machineries and technologies are needed and the problem may arise for harmonic performance of work through machineries to excavate out coal. The already practiced working modus operandi of workmen will be definitely a precedence to start up new functional mines with modern machineries of various parameters for same as well as different work.

While moving to the working mines even from the colonies, it was strictly instructed by the senior authorities to wear the helmet even inside the jeep as a precautionary measure. And this is mandatory for every person who enters the working mines.

And this provision is made to avoid all forms of risk and injury to the workmen of the mines. While leaving the residential colony and entering the mines the railway track was crossed by an over bridge. It was told by the expert that the working mines have its own small distance railway track to transport the excavated coal to the nearby thermal power plant (See Figure 14).

This reduces the transportation cost in long run of the operational mines. After crossing the railway bridge the "Artificial hill" which is also technically termed as "Over-burden" was seen. These "Over-Burden" hills are created by the excavated out soil over the coal chunk. Immediate after the end of the bridge on the left side while moving to the mines a running unit named as "Central Work Shop" is seen.

The "Central Work Shop" as told by experts is a Central junction of all the working mines of the NCL Project, where all the machineries come for repairing and maintenance.

The central workshop is a centre which enables to reduce the "Leads Time" of the maintenance of machineries. In the front of the "Central Work Shop" the obsolete spare parts are being displayed as an insignia of the working unit.

While moving to the pathway a ceremonial pond on left was found to be located in the periphery of the "Vocational Training Centre". The "Vocational Training Centre" is an organization which exercises the Training, Development and Refresher cum orientation courses for workmen of the NCL Company.

Figure 14. A location of opencast mines at NCL Jayant Project,
Singrauli, Madhya Pradesh

Further the Vocational Training Centre enables and prepares the workmen to make them competent enough to handle the various heavy machineries in working mines. It was told by experts that the smallest dumper has a capacity to transport a minimum of 85 tons of load at a time. And in present working mines in India the range of Dumpers in terms of capacity is from 85 tons to 210 tons. These heavy and extreme costly machineries are being operated by workmen of *"Excavation Cadre"*. It was very interesting to know that the minimum height of even smallest dumpers is equivalent to a 3 storey buildings height.

As told by experts, the tires of Dumpers do not have any tubes, as they are operated from vacuum pressure and known as "Tubeless tires". In technical terms as told by experts the Dumper is easier to be operated than to operate a "Video Game". The reason behind is the extreme high and sophisticated technology being induced in the machinery, which makes it the best transportation machinery for logistics movement of the mine products.

While preparing to finally enter into mines it was found the transit camp was surrounded by a deadline ropeway. The deadline ropeway is an indicative barrier which prohibits any individual to cross it, so as to avoid causality. But if any accident occurs beyond this line then no claim of compensation could be made on company. The transit camp is a junction which remains active 24 hours a day for change of duty shifts for workmen and also executive. The transit camp is affected with heavy noise pollution being made by the movement of heavy machineries. Finally it was indicated to the final moment to proceed to the working mines to capture the real tough and hazardous conditions of the workmen.

The walkie talkie was put on in continuous mode to be vigilant all around the mines for "Barrier free communication". These telecommunication gadgets are being maintained and being operated by *"Telecommunication Department Cadre".*

It was found that for the blasting purposes the explosives are being implanted by special compartmentalized trucks that use to fill the drilled holes with semi-viscous fluid technically called as "Sight Mixed Slurry". The same is mixed in a fixed proportion as per directions of the experts. The "Sight mixed Slurry" is handled by workmen of the *"Mining Cadre"* as per prescribed norms.

The drilled holes for the explosive are pierce in the working sites by the "Drilling Machine" and the same is being operated by workmen. The "Drilling Machine" is also monitored under portfolio of *"Excavation Cadre".* Prior a few minutes before blasting the heavy machines named as "Shovel" were being shifted to the safe position to avoid any damage due to blasting.

As told by the experts of the working mines the big machineries are being called by code names. The Shovel machines in the visited area were coded as "B-7" and "B-0". The works of these "Shovel" Machines are to load and off load the coal. The Shovel machine is monitored by workmen of *"Excavation Cadre".* The "Electrical and Mechanical Cadre" plays a crucial role in maintenance as well as providing continuous electricity supply and transformation to all machineries in mines as the location of machineries changes in 24-48 hours as per demands of coal chunk to be excavated out.

It was found that soon with help of indications and symbols by a workman the shovel operator marched to the safe position to assemble in secured zone. As a part of Instant planning it was found that the experts in the moving jeep gave instructions to have ample space to move dozers to proceed safely. Finally as a final check up the blasting site was visited.

It was found that a complete area of 50 square kilometers was packed with the explosives and connected with fuse wires and cast-boosters. In between the working mines the movement of the "Dragline" machine was observed. The "Dragline" machine is an extremely prestigious and world's third largest machine till date and is being used to excavate out the overburden soil as well as coal.

It was observed as well as later explained by the experts also that the "Dragline" machine which is the world's third largest working machine is continuous functional in working mines. This machinery use to get stopped for a few minutes to avoid any form of risk due to jerks caused from the explosions of the mines. The "Dragline" as told by experts costs on an average to 10-15 million US dollars in present global market.

Also the working mines of N.C.L. Singrauli have the highest number of "Dragline" machineries in comparison of all sister subsidiaries of Coal India. Also the "Dragline" in the company is being procured from U.S.A., Erstwhile U.S.S.R. and also from U.K. The movement of "Dragline" and other heavy machineries are coordinated with help of E-Governance in communication. As well as it is the best working reference of coordination and team work of Workmen in any industry. The "Dragline" machine is also monitored by "Excavation Cadre".

After the blast the workmen came out from the safety zone to the working zone and all the working machineries were found to get reactive in their work within five minutes after blasting. ***This is a positive shade of WPM that is the promptness of workmen***. Later the final clearance was made that every aspect related to security was confined to be secured.

At the end the working report were assimilated and the complete gist was verified for completion of report. This overview gist expresses the healthy status of "***Workers' Participation in Management in Policy Making***" as the policies are well executed as well as more healthy policies can be formulated for swift implementation. As well as a "no-causality" report was also counter verified. And finally one more security clearance was granted before the duty hour is declared to be finished. These steps of duty hours are exercised continuous for 24 hours all around the calendar year in phases of eight hours' shift of each. The "Dumper" comes under category "Non-Road Moving Vehicle".And for the same category a separate pathway is made in the working mines.

IMPORTANCE OF EXPERIENCE

The importance of experience of workmen was found after arrival of the hosts with welcome of hosts with "***Lemon Tea***". As a share of Experience statement from a workman it was told that "***Lemon Tea***" is being used all day so as to curtail out sleepiness and neuron-rigidity. Also if any stress is there then it is eliminated out. Also in addition to this a workmen spoke that "***Lemon Tea***" reduces chances of milk to be spoiled due to dust or heat of mines. The movement of machineries is majorly done by workmen following the working on the signal optics.

It was made aware by the working experts huge ammeters are being established to supply continuous uninterrupted electricity to the heavy machineries. Finally an intimation signal was given with help of lights to leave the place as soon blasting may take place. After the same the complete periphery of mines was rechecked by patrol of experts so that no accident may happen.

Regular and continuous exchange of reports and feedbacks to practice the security measure to avoid all forms of risk. This mechanism proves the concept of "Quality Circle" in practice with successful impact.

It was noticed that to work in the blasting region is one of the most risky and robust form of work. It was told by the experts that the present explosive Sight mixed slurry is multi times more powerful than traditional explosives as Dynamite and RDX.

In the final moment the clearance and recheck up was made in a periphery of 500 meters so that no one may remain in the blasting zone. It was found to be a very hard humanistic condition for work for the complete cycle of preparation for the blasting for the coal excavation. After the complete check up the blasting took place and the complete area of 50 square meters was blown up. It was observed that the machineries were placed at safe positions as to avoid any form of risk of damage to the machineries.

The coal is the support line of the energy production in India presently and it will be the biggest source of energy production till the substitute of energy is found. The energy especially in form of electricity is the prime form of energy provider to all the jurisdiction of industries and agriculture.

The Indian agriculture is mass supported by the proper irrigation and water to cultivate lands. And the prime source of electricity production is coal. For the same all life lines are directly or indirectly dependent on the coal industry in present era.

In the environment where the atmospheric temperature was 22 degree Celsius it was found that the temperature of mines was 34 degree Celsius. This is a very hard and realistic working conditions being faced by the workmen. Further the "Experience Reckoning" of workmen can be an important tool to impart training to new workmen recruited for handling heavy machineries in new working mines to be operated.

More explorative research can bring out more feasible policies and methodologies by which the performance of workmen will be more secured and productive. The feedback collection and experience record of workmen who operate same machineries as well as different machineries will be a fruitful outcome to enhance the work performance of workmen in opencast mines. (See Figure 15).

Figure 15. A workman at opencast mines of NCL Jayant,
Singrauli Project, Madhya Pradesh.

As told by the experts that in every subsidiaries of Coal India, the working mines are now dependent in automated machineries in opencast as well as underground mines.

The fully mechanized machineries as "Dumpers", "Dozer", "Shovel", and "Girder" in the mines are operated by "Workers". The proper training at "Vocational Training" Centre enables the "Workmen" to operate these extreme huge machineries to perform smoothly. The experts also told that the cost of one single machine costs between 800 to 1000 million INR. And the cost increases with increase in capacity of machineries.

These machineries use to work almost 24 hours a day in different shift. The total number of machineries varies from different subsidiaries to subsidiaries as per requirement and nature of mining operations (See Statistical Table 1 to Statistical Table 5).

As told by experts The "Dumper" is costs 1200 to 1500 million INR and it is almost 3-4 times heavy than a battle tank in weight. And it needs a lot of experience and balance to operate such heavy and costly machineries in the working mines. Also it was made to be known by experts that a single "Dragline: machine cost 8000 to 12000 million INR.

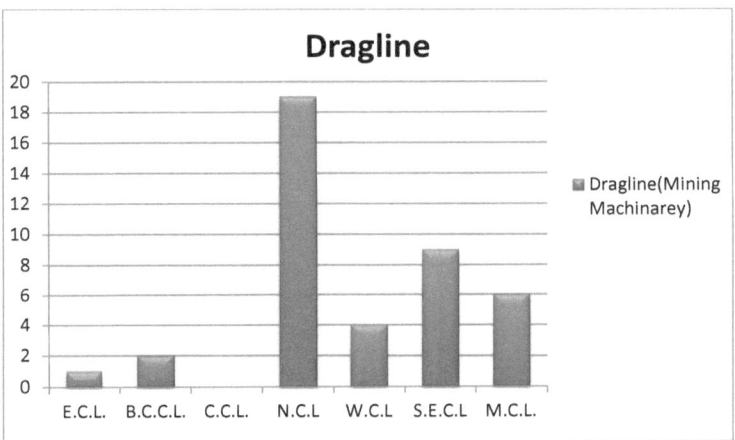

Statistical Table Number – 1.

A comparative statistical representation of Dragline Machineryin

all nine sister subsidiaries of Coal India Limited.

Source:- Angar Monthly Newsletter,

Indian Institute of Coal Management, March 2008, Edition-11, Page-2

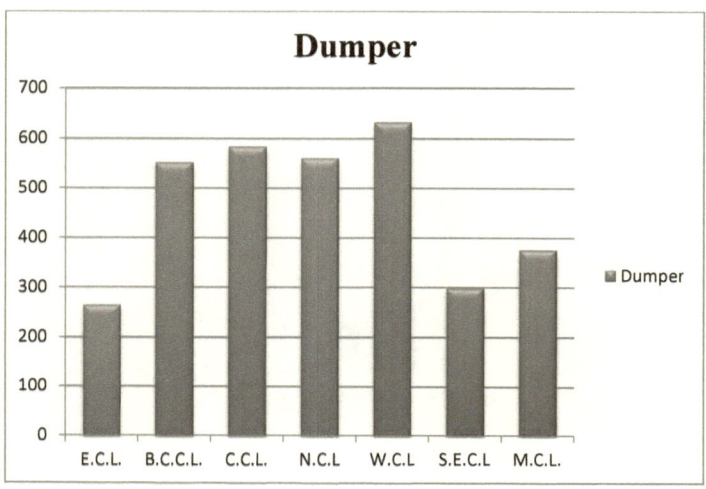

Statistical Table Number – 2.

A comparative statistical representation of Dumper in all nine sister subsidiaries of Coal India Limited. Source:- Angar Monthly Newsletter, Indian Institute of Coal Management, March 2008, Edition-11, Page-2

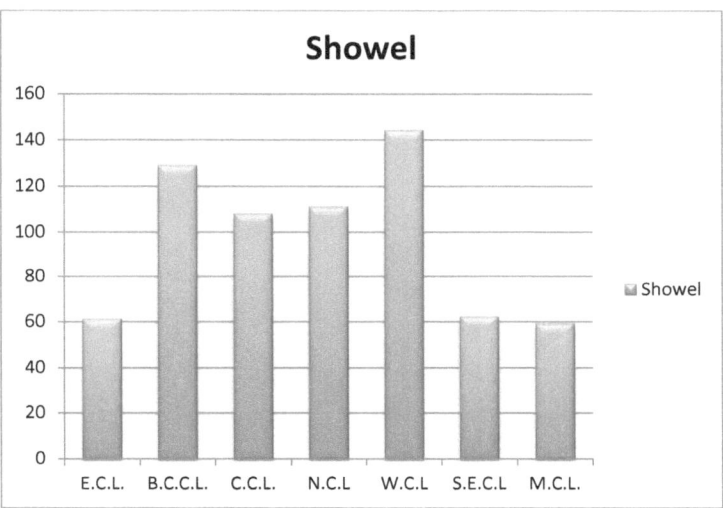

Statistical Table Number – 3.

A comparative statistical representation of Showel Machinery

in all nine sister subsidiaries of Coal India Limited.

Source:- Angar Monthly News letter,

Indian Institute of Coal Management, March 2008, Edition-11, Page-2

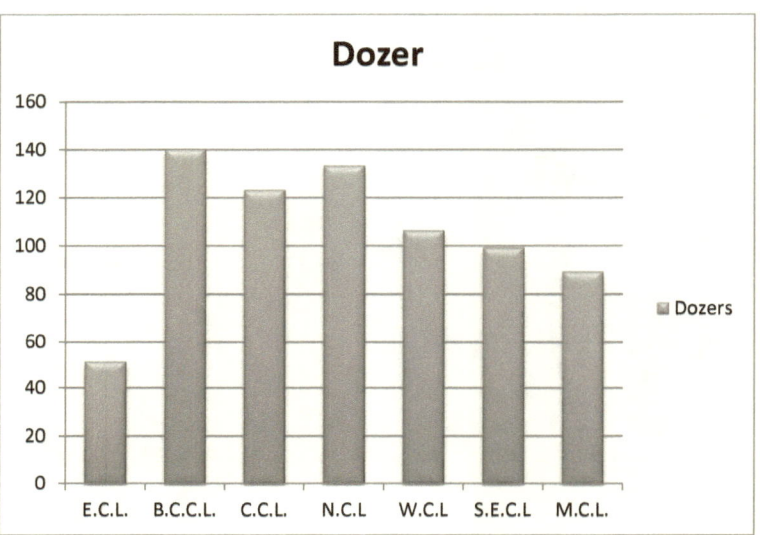

Statistical Table Number – 4.

A comparative statistical representation of Dozer Machinery

in all nine sister subsidiaries of Coal India Limited.

Source:- Angar Monthly Newsletter

,Indian Institute of Coal Management, March 2008, Edition-11, Page-2

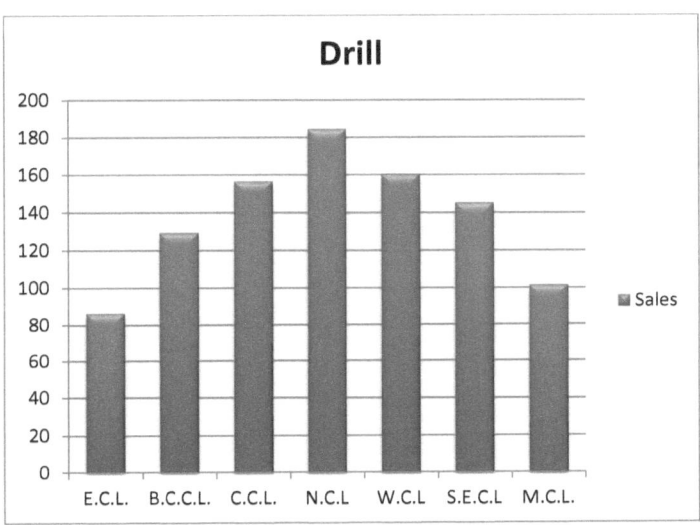

Statistical Table Number – 5.

A comparative statistical representation of Drill Machine

in all nine sister subsidiaries of Coal India Limited.

Source:- Angar Monthly Newsletter,

Indian Institute of Coal Management, March 2008, Edition-11, Page-2

REFERENCES

1. Pahariya NC, Shrivastava, Abhinav Kumar, "Exercise Of Cadre Coordination By Workmen By Virtue Of Proper Training At Open Cast Mines At Northern Coalfields Limited, Singrauli (Madhya Pradesh)", International Journal of Research in Commerce, Economics and Management, Volume No.(02),2012, Issue No.09 (September), ISSN 2231-4245.

CHAPTER#7

WPM in Enhancing Quality of work life

The quality of worklife for workmen is the most important factor to be strengthened and uplifted. Water is the most important element for all Industries to perform smoothly and efficiently. Water is the ingredient of ensuring the better Quality of Work life for working personnel. Further all the "**Core Sector Industries**" are fully dependent on water for their efficient performance for contribution to the Gross Domestic Production of National Economy. **Article 21** of Constitution of India states the "**Right to Life**" is a constitutional right to every citizen of India. For the same all elements which are the basic needs to lead the life are provided under constitutional umbrella.

Blessed to be a prime mineral belt the geography of Dhanbad is similar to a Peninsula which is surrounded by water from three sides. In North is in touch with Maithon Dam, a reservoir for hydro electricity. In south it is River Damodar and in west it is touching the beds of River Barakar. The demography of Dhanbad is a fusion or rural and urban both in a composite scale. As many developed portions are in cluster of developed colonies and many large population are residing in the rural areas of the District of Dhanbad.

But still the crisis of Drinking water is prevailing at a high scale in surroundings of Dhanbad. The main reasons for water crisis are lack of technological re-engineering, weak administrative control of local law and order, delay in implementation of policies. These all results the water crisis for drinking as well as for the Industrial demands too.

The crisis of Drinking water is prevailing at a high scale in surroundings of Dhanbad. The Dhanbad coal Belt produces the finest form of coking coal for the production of steel of Bokaro Steel Processing Plant which is located at a distance of the 30 Kilometre from the operational coal mines of Dhanbad.

The Produced coking coal is being washed before being sent to the Steel Processing Industry. The enormous water is being consumed to wash the coking coal to settle down the dust particles of the coal. The produced coal is washed with heavy splash of water before the coal being dispatched to the Steel Plants. The water left after use is called as "**Middling**" of washery coal water. And the same "**Middling**" is released in river Damodar and Barakar. And this pollutes the river water.

Though the water finally flows in Bay of Bengal but still the particles hampers the filtration process by making heavy damages to drinking water supply. Also the dust granules hamper the filtration process by making heavy damages to filtration pumps. Further the underground water comes in a huge amount from the coal being excavated out from the coal being excavated out from underground pits working mines. This water is mixture of many minerals diluted in water. Generally this water is named as "**Dung Water**" by local people but in actual state it is mineral full water.

This water is extremely enriching for crops and farming after minor filtration and little processing with chemicals. On the other hand this water is extremely dangerous for human consumption. Unfortunately still thousands of people are still daily being dependent on this water. This water has already affected lives of thousands of people in nearby area. Generally people use to get "**Gastro-Intestinal Disorder**" and "Urinary Disorders" too at a large scale.

In a ground level field survey it was found that the supply pipelines are being intentionally being broken even after regular repair by the local anti-social elements. The prime motto is to collect water from the broken pipes and then to resell it. These shroud mentality of local inhabitants has created a lot of problem for the supply of the drinking water.

In addition to this the local people also don't want to get these pipeline repaired as their source of income will be surely snatched. While interviewing a man filling water, he replied that if the pipelines would be repaired then he would be in loss as due to the same his livelihood will be snatched as he can't resell the water coming out from the broken pipes. So they don't want it to be repaired. It has been identified by visiting field that in a single kilometer there are almost 30-40 pipeline breakages.

These are the major cause of slow speed of flow of the water. In addition to this the water uses to get contaminated due to the same. And it cause occasionally multiple numbers of health causalities due to epidemic. Many times the huge pipelines are being broken even before they are implanted by the local people. For the same these pipes are being kept in nearby periphery of local Police stations so that no locals may disturb them (See Figure 16).

The same situation was found in the locality of Kenduadih, where the hundreds of pipes which are to be implanted for maintenance of the broken pipes are kept in secured portfolio of local Kendudih Police Station of Dhanbad District. This expresses the fear and weakness of local administration from the anti social elements that may create sabotage.

Figure 16. The water supply pipelines kept near Kenduadih
Police station for safety against any sabotage.

The key problems which arise due to shortage of water are as follows:-

1. Due to scarcity of water, a number of strikes and "Gheraos" are happening and it leads to a tremendous loss to overall profit of the organization (Coal India).
2. A sudden blockade use to occur in day to day work due to scarcity of drinking water.
3. A huge sum has to be paid by the local people to buy water.
4. Ample water is available for drinking consumption as well as for Industrial needs, only strategically swift water resource management policies are to be framed and implemented.
5. The population residing in local region turns volatile many times due to continuous shortage of water. This results into conflict which finally ends up with huge financial loss to company.

A FEASIBLE SOLUTION

The "Rain-Water Harvesting" and "Recycling of Waste Water" are two options which are very feasible for uplifting the Quality of Life of workmen, especially in "Core-Sector" Industries.

While my visit to Sri Lanka I found "Integrated Colonies" for workmen using "Water conservation".

WASTE WATER USE CATEGORIZATION

Wastewater reuse can be categorized by its sources, benefits, application and required treatments.

Wastewater reuse is divided by its source into[2].

- *Gray Water reuse*: Untreated household wastewater that has not come in contact with toilet waste and include wastewater from bathtub, showers washbasins, clothes washing machine and laundry tubs, but does not include wastewater from kitchen sinks or dishwashers or laundry water from washing of material soiled with human excreta, such as diapers
- *Effluent reuse*: The effluent from waste water treatment plants can be used for various purpose ranging from urban, Agriculture, and environmental to potable purpose depending on the level of treatment the effluent is subjected to.
- Industrial process water reuse.
- Rain water

BENEFITS OF WATER RECYCLING

- Recharges ground water.
- Replenishes surface water bodies.
- Supplements potable water for non potable uses.
- To make a new in house, reliable water source available.
- reduction in fresh water cost
- Reduction in disposal cases.
- An approach towards zero liquid discharge.
- Protection of environment.
- Effectively combat the water scarcity.

REFERENCES

1) Pahariya NC, Shrivastava, Abhinav Kumar, Water Crisis At Coal Capital Of India:-A Pragmatic Study Of Root Causes, Impact And Solution Of Water Crisis In Regions Of Working Coal Mines Of Bharat Coking Coal Limited Dhanbad", International Journal of Research in Commerce, IT and Management, Volume No.(02),2012, Issue No.09 (September), ISSN 2231-5756.

2) Shrivastava Abhinav Kumar, Excerpts from the Final Project Report of data collection work for Ph.D Research Topic titled "Workers' Participation in Management in Policy Making"; Submitted at Ministry of Water Supply and Drainage, Government of Sri Lanka, Colombo vide Certification Number "3/1/7/79" dated 03.02.2012

CHAPTER#8

WPM as a Constructive Positive Pressure Group in Organization

The BCCL Company was a financially a huge loss making company since its nationalization upto the financial year 2005-2006. This success was due to the "Turn-Key" effect of the "Electronic-Auction" scheme introduced for procurement of coal. The scheme of Electronic Auction is also conferred as "E-Auction".

The BCCL Company is the 1st Public Sector Undertaking which started *E-Auction in the Energy Sector in India.* Electronic-Auction started in the month of January 2005. The E-Auction is governed by sales control and planning Department. E-Auction turned the BCCL Company into a profit giving company in matter of revenue for the first time since last 30 years. (See Diagram 4)

E-Auctioning made the company out of the financial loss and The annual financial profit for the Year 2005-2006 of the Bharat Coking Coal Limited Company was 228 crore. The purpose of E-Auction is to provide equal opportunity to purchase coal through single window service to all intending buyers.

E-Auction has been introduced to facilitate across the country wide Ranging access to book coal on line for all sections of coal Buyers enabling them to buy coal through a simple transparent and consumer friendly system of marketing and distribution of coal all over territories of India. (See Diagram 5)

A Diagrammatic Representation of Progressive Impact of the Electronic – Auction (E-Auction) on the overall expansion of the BCCL Company as well as the Coal India Limited Company.

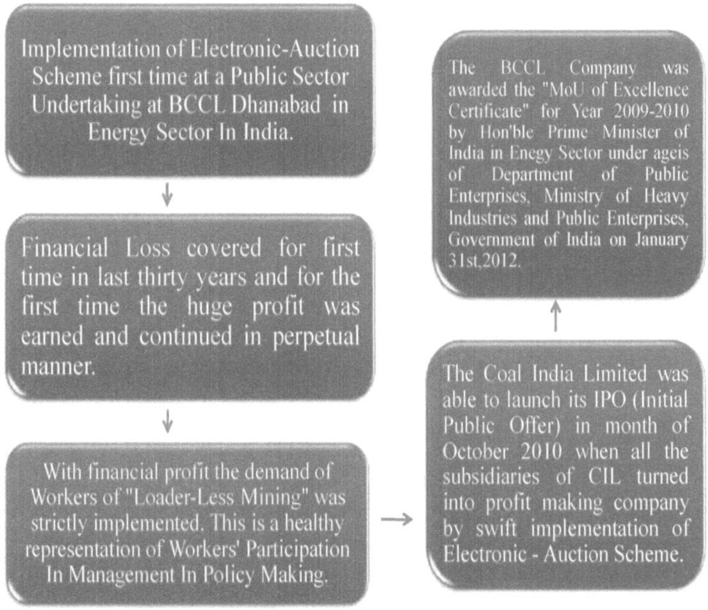

Implementation of Electronic-Auction Scheme first time at a Public Sector Undertaking at BCCL Dhanabad in Energy Sector In India.

The BCCL Company was awarded the "MoU of Excellence Certificate" for Year 2009-2010 by Hon'ble Prime Minister of India in Enegy Sector under ageis of Department of Public Enterprises, Ministry of Heavy Industries and Public Enterprises, Government of India on January 31st,2012.

Financial Loss covered for first time in last thirty years and for the first time the huge profit was earned and continued in perpetual manner.

The Coal India Limited was able to launch its IPO (Initial Public Offer) in month of October 2010 when all the subsidiaries of CIL turned into profit making company by swift implementation of Electronic - Auction Scheme.

With financial profit the demand of Workers of "Loader-Less Mining" was strictly implemented. This is a healthy representation of Workers' Participation In Management In Policy Making.

Diagram:- 4

Source:- "Angar" Monthly Journal, January 2011,Volume 1; Page-3,published and distributed by I.I.C.M. Ranchi (Indian Institute of Coal Management, Ranchi)

Abhinav Kumar Shrivastava

A COMPARITIVE REPRESENTATION OF THE SALES OF COAL BEFORE AND AFTER LAUNCH OF E-AUCTION (PER TON) IN INR

Sl No.	Bid Value of Coal	Minimum Bid Value of Coal	Maximum Bid Value of Coal Before E-Auction (Average per ton)	Maximum Bid Value of Coal After E-Auction (Average per ton)	Average Profit after E-Auction (Average per ton)
01.	1000.00	1000.00	1000.00	18500.00 - 22500.00	19500-22000.00

Diagram 5. A Hypothetical Statstical Representing the comparative status of profit earning from sales of Coal before and after implementation of E-Auction Scheme.

It is found that the E-Auction procedure is the only "Turn-Key" factor which covered the loss gaps and created an environment of financial profit with perpetual growth. The success of E-Auction at BCCL, Dhanbad has accelerated the launch of E-Auction Scheme in the entire sister subsidiaries of Coal India Limited. In addition as the most important segment of *Workers' Participation in Management in Policy Making*, the demand for the "**Loader less Mining**" in underground coal mining was put up in demand about 20 years back In this mechanism no worker will be excavating out any form of coal in underground mines with their own hand. All works have to be done only with help of machineries.

This concept was under the red-tapism due to shortage of funds and hence was delayed. As the machineries to be procured for the underground coal mining by help of "Loader-Less Mining" are extremely sophisticated and too costly too.

It was again demanded in the NCWA-VIII National Coal Wage Agreement-VIII. As a *"Positive Pressure Group"* the representative bodies demanded this provision to be true in sense of implementation when policy of *"Loader less Mining"* and it was smoothly implemented on 01.04.2009 on the working grounds of all functional underground mines in B.C.C.L. Dhanbad.

This action was a big transformative step with an absolute *"Humantic Touch"* of the Management. And this has been possible with diplomatic and strong approach of representative body of workers as well as the demands of the workers' representative to invest the financial profit earned due to swift implementation of E-Auction Scheme.

This action also acted as a motivating factor for workers to create an atmosphere of enthusiasm and more dedication for work. This has also empowered the scenario of *"Zero Accident Atmosphere"*. This step of management has made the concept of *"Accident Free"* mines true upto maximum.

This has made an inner motivation for both the workers; the underground workers as well as the upper-surface workers to work full more enthusiasm. This has been made possible in practical due to *"Collective bargaining with a positive attitude"* for a situation of win-win for both the management as well as workers.

In a chain mechanism it was observed that the financial profit was made due to swift and secured Implementation of E-Auction, the same financial profit was invested in procuring the most modern machineries of mines to implement the **"Loader-Less Mining"**.

These all stepwise mechanism enabled the BCCL Company to receive the honor of award of the "MoU Excellence Certificate" for year 2009-2010 by Dr. Manamohan Singh, Honorable Prime Minister of India on 31st January 2012 at New Delhi, under aegis of Department of Public Enterprises, Ministry of Heavy Industries and Public Enterprises, Government of India (See Figure 18).

As a few other subsidiaries were also in loss from last few years for the same the CIL was unable to represent it as an overall profit making company. Along with the BCCL company the E-Auction scheme was launched in the entire nine sister subsidiaries, including the loss making as well as the profit making companies. This scheme turned the loss making companies to cover the loss and profit making companies as well as the profit making companies turned to "*Super-Abnormal Profit*" making companies. And policy of "Loader Less mining" in exercise has become a boon for the underground mines workmen (See Figure 19). And on an aggregate scale the CIL became a profit making company. In order of expansion to be a "*Global Giant*" in Core Sector Energy Industries the CIL launched its IPO Initial Public Offer on October 18th, 2010 in open market.

The source step cause of profit earning was launch of E-Auction. The channelized co-ordination of policy and vision has created this tremendous developmental change in the BCCL as well as CIL and its subsidiaries too.

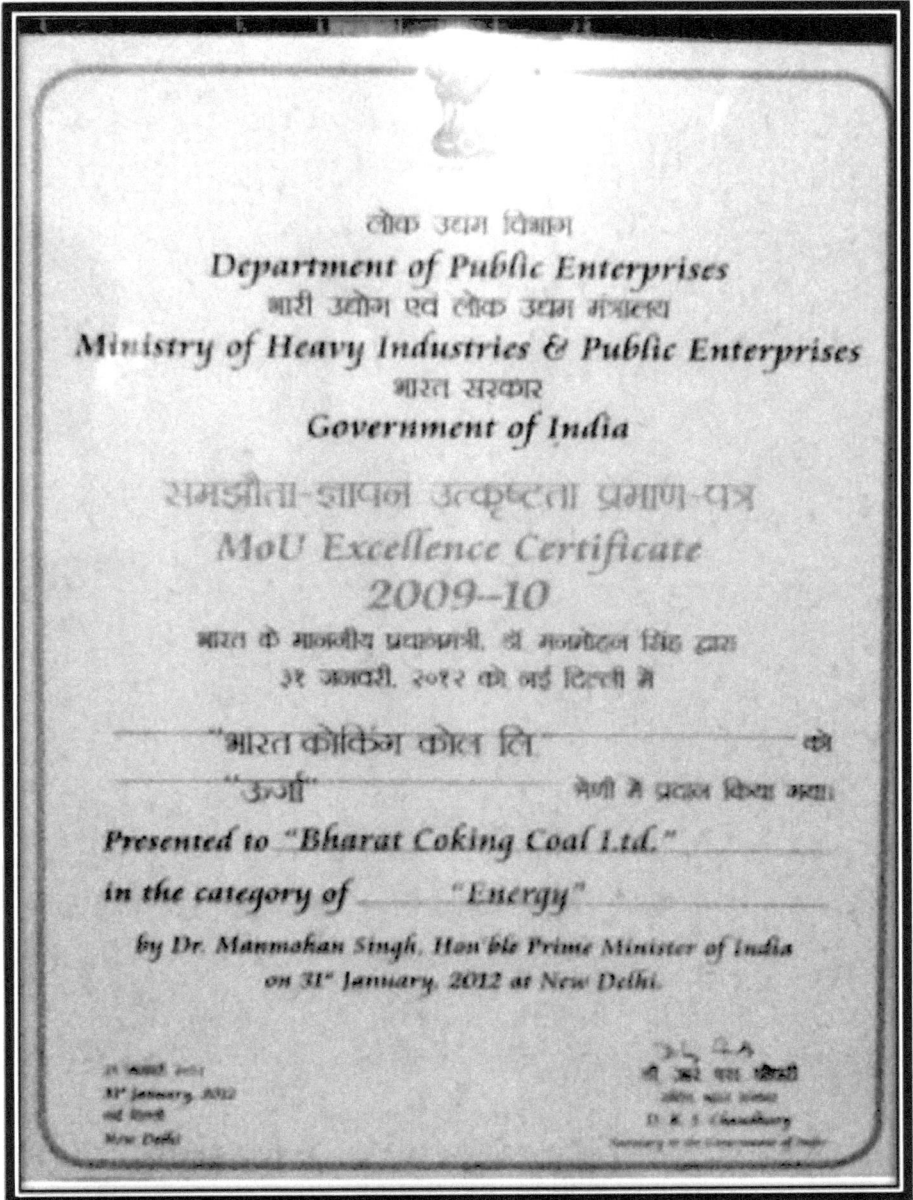

Figure 17 Source :- Public Photo Gallery, Labour's Day
(May 01,2012), Koyla Bhawan, BCCL, Dhanbad.

Figure 18. Well equipped workmen with safety gadgets and Occupational
Safety Dress code going to duty in underground mines.
These underground mines are now in active operating state with
"Loader-Less Mining" creating "Zero Accident Zone" for workmen.

REFERENCES

1) Pahariya NC, Shrivastava, Abhinav Kumar, Electronic Auction: - A Turn-Key Factor To Rejuvenate The Coal Industry: - A Case Study Of Bharat Coking Coal Limited, Dhanbad, International Journal of Research in Computer Application and Management, Volume No.(02),2012, Issue No.09 (September), ISSN 2231-1009.

CHAPTER#9

Graphology in WPM

ETHICAL PREFACE

At the time of Pre Thesis Seminar for Ph.D, my Research showcase on Graphology was curtailed out!! The rationale given was that Graphology is an "Applied Clinical Psychology" stream and it has no relevance with core labor issue. I told that it is much helpful in "Industrial Relations" and "Group Dynamics". But No means No by some "Excellent Problem Makers" during Pre Thesis Seminar.

On that day I decided that I will melt my hard work on Graphology in form of a book to reach maximum audience. And here I am!! Also why I must be afraid to present of my real hard work? The research and innovation is the prime factor for growth of well being of society. And then I made a healthy attempt to create a new horizon in "Human Impact Assessment". Please find Enclosures of my hard work on consistent effort on Graphology in "Annexure F" to "Annexure I"

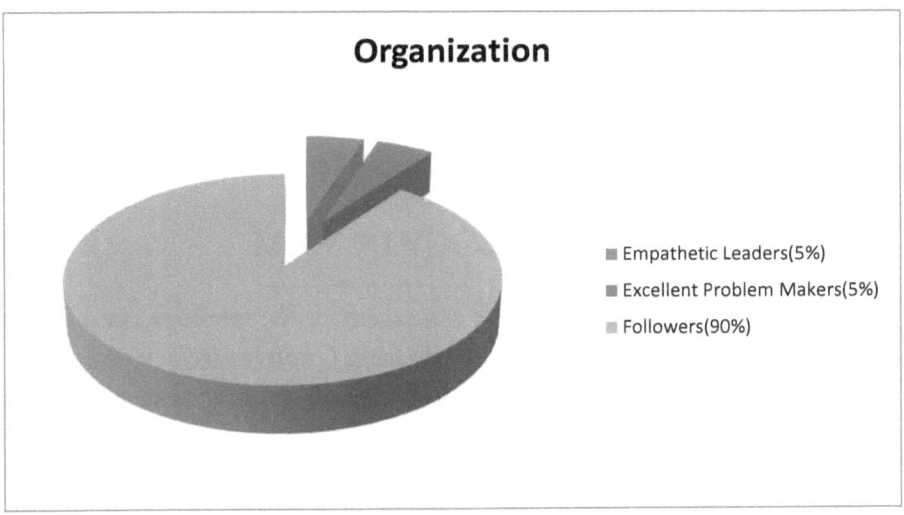

A Representation of my view of Mentality of People in Organization.

INTRODUCTION

Graphology is an ancient scientific art which interprets the behavior, attitude, strength, weakness, likes, dislikes of an individual by individual's handwriting. It reads the psychological state of mind uncover out the hidden talent in Human Being. Also it is a well said proverb that "**Nature & Signature**" never changes. And in current pace of global Business environment Graphology can be used as "**Supersonic Catalyst**" tool to get assured success [1].

SCIENTIFIC SUPPORT

The shorthand writing style, musical tunes symbols and "Electro-cardiogram" are some scientific proofs where the symbols are being understood and interpreted.

Graphology gives the "Midas-Touch" to the HRD and Manpower planning of any organization. There are millions of languages in this world which neither are till date nor understood nor interpretable. Similarly the reading of Graphology must also be more and more enhanced to get the best outcomes.

LEGAL SUPPORT

Section 45 of Evidence Act 1878 approves the "Handwriting Expert's" view as a legal subject.

GRAPHOLOGY IN WPM

In portfolio of Human Recourse Management, Graphology can be used at tactical and decision making level for creating ***Quality circle***. It's extremely difficult to use Graphology for huge number of labor force engaged in policy making and collective bargaining.

As due to the large number of population as well as illiteracy and non acquaintance with English language of the Labor force. As the present Graphology is limited to Latin alphabets only.

But at the managerial level Graphology can be used among educated executives to identify the social, empathetic and unbiased representatives among executives. This may generate creative flexibility among negotiators for communication dialogue on behalf of management.

And about a dozen clusters of 3-4 representatives each will be definitely enough to negotiate to solve all forms of industrial and labor disputes as well as framing of the policies in industries from size of 500 workmen to one million workmen. Further the number of clusters of representatives may be increased or decreased as per requirements in very short notice of time.

This will definitely smooth the process of exchange of ideas and opinions for formulation and making of policy. As well as it will enhance the share of ***Workers Participation in Management in policy making*** from the side of management with more active participation.

WORKING OF RAINBOW ANALYSIS OF GRAPHOLOGY

The Expert Graphologist [2] recommends the following unique process for accurate interpretation by Graphology. They are as follows [3]:-

1) The Handwriting Sample of Candidate with Consent Form from client. The Written Documents are separated in different segments of Outline Drawing, Sketches without colors, Signatures, Figures, Digits and Special Symbols. The sample is taken in supporting Environment Acoustics on special designed sheets with recommended Pen by Expert Graphologist.

2) The initial Analysis for identification of Alphabets covers a minimum 60-90 hours. Every alphabet and symbol is processed and analyzed very deliberately. Then A minimum of 85-100 photocopies of written samples are taken for marking the various codes for processing without making any change in initial sample document.

3) The profiled and separated alphabets are analyzed separately with various "Secret Codes" assigned by Expert Graphologist. The result of all alphabets are coded and compiled to make a complete gist. Thrice the recertification is done for the collected samples' result before the complete drafting.

4) The verified alphabetic codes are manipulated with the assigned "Secret Interpretation" by Expert Graphologist. Final Format is made ready with elaborated explanation in three colors, viz Red, Green and Blue.

5) The Green Color represents the Positive Qualities, The Blue marks the hidden potential not being used and Red symbolizes the negative factor to be eliminated.

6) The report is handed over to the client in person. Explanation and Doubt clearance from client within 7 days is collected. The final counseling of 45-60 minutes is served to client for complete elaboration of all samples collected.

7) The sample collected is returned with interpreted report to the client. The Photocopies of samples are destroyed in a secured Environment Friendly manner. The same is done for absolute Secrecy of client's sample so that the writing samples may not be misused.

REFERENCES

1) *Pahariya NC, Chowhan SS, Shrivastava AK, Graphology: A Concealed Tool for Creation and Development of Human Resource Capital, Review of HRM Vol. 1, No. 4, April-June 2012, ISSN- 2249-4650.*

2) *Original thoughts of Dr. Abhinav Kumar Shrivastava, A Common Honest and Ethical Indian, Identity: - Indian Passport Identity number "H 9 7 9 5 1 1 4".*

3) *Shrivastava AK, Workers' Participation in Management in Policy Making: - Roots and Routes for Prosperous Industrialized Economy, LAP Lambert Publication, Germany, ISBN: - 978-3-659-35799-2, Pp167-178*

CHAPTER#10

Future of WPM

The Proposed Future Paradigm:-
The "Institutionalization Model of WPM"

The new proposed model of **"Institutionalization Model of WPM"** is developed and arranged with objective to get every drop of information with a synergistic approach so as to empower the healthy democratic representation in all spheres of management and workmen of the industries[1]. The proposed model is recommended to be recognized as **"Future of WPM"** in global scenario with comparison to present context and status of WPM in implantation as well as in progress pipeline all around the globe.

With growing needs and demands of the industrial expansion all over the globe the role of workmen in industry has increased significantly. The response from workmen have proven its' strong impact on the surface of the industry. The feedback mechanism is amalgamated with change agents which evolutes a new model on modern managerial segment. A well said proverb supports the model that "An individual is best judge for oneself". With the same rationale the new model is proposed. As the workmen and other personnel know their own capacity and present situation very well.

Workmen themselves only can express their problems, needs, developmental demands, professional safety, occupational hazards and their diversion and mitigation and other progressive facets of their day to day life. Any healthy institution all around globe is neutral, committed to assist and help, unbiased and pro-mentoring in nature. The culture of any organization depends upon the behavior of working personnel.

With more and more participation the culture of company turns to be more "Participative Culture". As well as the feeling of belongingness and empathy develops in mindset of workmen. These feelings propagate the inner motivation among workmen to work more dedicatedly and the same results into higher production and profitable output.

In order to make an absolute balance between workmen and management the proposed paradigm of "*Institutionalization Model of WPM*" is framed. This proposed model is in cyclic order and is segmented into three *different parts* consisting of total of nine steps.

The following three phases(Part-"A", Part "B", Part "C" respectively) will elaborate in a more crystal clear representation about the proposed model of WPM in Policy making:

PART "A".

a) **Collection of Feedback from Workmen**: - The response and the feedback from workmen is the most important information which can be further processed for developmental policies. But outmost care must be taken to collect the feedback so that maximum information can be gathered.

b) **Experience Reckoning count and Processing:** - The day to day of working of workmen results into a lot of experience gaining of the workmen. These experiences can be very useful in making further developmental policies. Collection of Experience will result into huge stockpile of data. Many data may be useless or may have been suggested earlier. For the same with the processing the unwanted data must be separated out.

c) **Identification of Professional Hazards:** - The workmen engaged in daily working activity can sense the movement of machineries and equipments very easily with their experience. With the early identification of hazards the risks can be easily curtailed and curbed down as well as preparedness policies can be well formulated in anticipation. These keep a regular checks and balances to suppress all forms of risk at nascent level only.

d) **Suggestion for Feasible Steps to be adopted:-** The suggestions from all the corners must be always welcomed. But only those suggestions must be accepted which are economically feasible and are also permissible as per law of Land.

PART "B"

a) **Feedback Processing:-** From all the steps of Part "A" above stated the feedbacks must be directly and separately send to a common junction for feedback processing. The feedback processing will scrutinize the required feedback in form of data and will finally extract the required filtered information.

b) **Legal Audit:-** The filtered feedback data must be then processed with scanning of legal audit. This is mandatory for satisfying the requirements of law of land, local and provincial ordnances and rules, to follow the laws as well as to check that any legal boundaries must not be crossed.

And at the end it must also not go against International Organization, Conventions and Laws. Few examples of International Conventions and Laws are "International Labor Organization", "Kyoto Protocol", and "Copenhagen Summit 2009".

c) **Social and Economic Impact Assessment:-** Any organization directly or indirectly is dependent on society and environment as well as also responsible for both society and environment. For the same it must be taken out most care that the policies going to get framed must not make any disturbance or imbalance towards society and environment.

d) **Policy Making:-** With final analysis of all the steps the final policy making must be done.

PART "C"

a) **Policy Implementation:** - The last step is for the final execution of policy framed. As well as with the policy execution the feedback box must also be connected. This is suggested to be done to make a complete cyclic rotation with regular frequency interval in organization.

The total cycle of work is from initial collection of feedback to final policy implementation is strongly recommended to be completed in duration of 30-45 days.

As well as this working of Institutionalization model must be exercised regularly with maximum gap duration of six months.(Please refer Diagram 3)

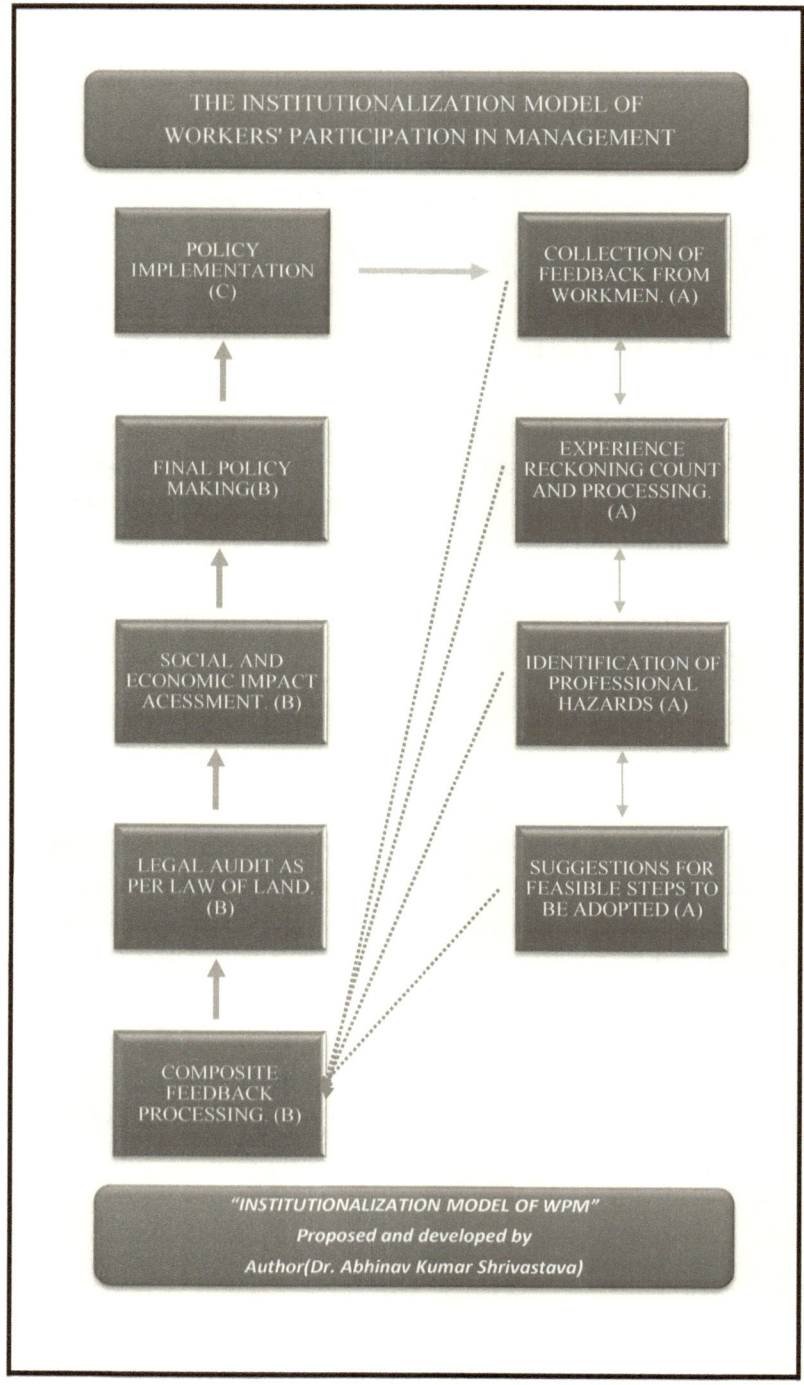

EXPECTED KEY OUT COMES.

The Expected Key Outcomes of "Institutionalization Model of WPM" are as follows:-

1. Higher Level of Participation.
2. Developmental and Progressive Change.
3. Internal Empowerment of Organization.
4. Strengthen of Healthy Industrial Democracy.
5. Enhancing the swift mechanism of Disputes Settlement.
6. Generation of more job opportunities in various stages of the "Institutionalization Model of WPM".
7. Regular updating of the Professional Work Environment for strengthening and expansion of organization.
8. Creation of "Empathetic Behavior" and generation of "Feeling of Belongingness" among workmen towards the company.
9. Enhancing of more dedication and motivation among workmen towards their work as well as their parent company too.

PROPOSED RECOMMENDATIONS

1) Institutionalization model of WPM must be made mandatory at every industry which involves large manpower in form of workmen, personnel as well as executive.
2) The working members of Institutionalization Model of WPM must be picked from every portfolio of the organization. This will segregate the various expertise on a single Platform with dissemination of successful outcome with "***Superfine Perfection***" as a healthy symbol of Industrial Heritage.

REFERENCES

1. Shrivastava, Abhinav Kumar, Institutionalization Model of Workers' Participation in Management in Policy Making, International Journal of Computer Science & Management Studies, Vol. 13, Issue 05, July 2013.

2. Shrivastava AK, Workers' Participation in Management in Policy Making: - Roots and Routes for Prosperous Industrialized Economy, LAP Lambert Publication, Germany, ISBN: - 978-3-659-35799-2, Pp 140-147

CHAPTER#11

Annexures

ANNEXURE "A"

BHARAT COKING COAL LIMITED
(A subsidiary of Coal India Limited)
OFFICE OF THE GENERAL MANAGER
HUMAN RESOURCE DEVELOPMENT DEPARTMENT
KALYAN BHAWAN, JAGJIVAN NAGAR, DHANBAD

Ref: BCCL/GM (HRD)/NIMS/RES.TRG/2011/ **1563**   Date: 16ᵗʰ Sept/2011

To
The General Manager (P&IR)
B.C.C.L.
Koyla Bhawan.

Sub: Six weeks unpaid PhD. Research work on topic "Worker's Participation in
Management in Policy Making" by a PhD Research Scholar of NIMS
University, Shobhanagar, Jaipur-303121.

Dear Sir,

With reference to above, Mr. **Abhinav Kumar Shrivastava** a Phd. Research Scholar in Management of **NIMS University, Shobha Nagar Jaipur - 303121** is hereby allowed to carry out a research work in your department for six weeks' period commencing **from 16th September 2011.** Subject to following terms & Conditions:

1. He cannot claim any employment in BCCL on basis of this training.
2. In case of any accident during his training period BCCL will not be responsible for any compensation.
3. No financial assistance will be paid to him nor any financial assistance will be borne by BCCL.
4. He has to arrange his own accommodation transport etc.
5. He has to sign and submit indemnity Bond duly registered by Notary Public.
6. He has to submit two duly attested passport size photographs.
7. Only Published information shall be provided, if needed.
8. A copy of collected data/ information in form of a project report shall be submitted before publication in P&IR and HRD Departments.
9. The candidate will be submitting a copy of the PhD Thesis after award of his PhD degree at P&IR and HRD Departments.
10. No extension of training will be granted.

I am directed to request you to kindly extend necessary research facilities to him without effecting normal activities of the department and put his under concerned officer for necessary guidance etc. It may kindly be noted that the student has submitted the Indemnity bond duly registered by Notary Public in the HRD Department.

His training shall be terminated automatically after completion of aforesaid period.

This has approval of the Competent Authority.

Yours faithfully

(R.N. Vishwakarma)
Sr. Manager (Mining)

Copy to:
1. Person Concerned.
2. General Manager (HRD), BCCL, Kalyan Bhawan.
3. TS to D (P), BCCL, Koyla Bhawan.
4. Prof. (Dr.) N C Pasriya, Dean Research NIMS University, Shobha Nagar Jaipur - 303121

BCCL

ANNEXURE "B"

भारत कोकिंग कोल लिमिटेड
BHARAT COKING COAL LIMITED
(कोल इण्डिया लिमिटेड का एक अंग)
(A Subsidiary of Coal India Limited)
कार्मिक निदेशालय
Personnel Directorate

कोयला भवन
Koyla Bhawan
कोयला नगर
Koyla Nagar
धनबाद -826005
Dhanbad-826005

Ref.No.BCCL:GM(P&IR):Sr.ES:11: 324   Dated:31.10.2011

The Sr.Manager(Mining)(HRD)
HRD Complex
Kalyan Bhawan,
Dhanbad.

Sub: six weeks un-paid research work.

Dear Sir,

In pursuance of your letter No.BCCL:GM(HRD)/NIMS:RES:TRG :2011/1563 dated 16th September, 2011, Mr. Abhinav Kumar Srivastava, student of a Phd. Reasearch Schlar in Management of NIMS University, Shobha Nagar, Jaipur-303121 reported to this office on 17.09.2011 for his six weeks unpaid research work on "Worker's Participation in Management in Policy Making"

Necessary assistance & guidance has been extended to him and he has completed his six weeks unpaid research work on "Worker's Participation in Management in Policy Making successfully.

This is for your information & further necessary action.

Yours faithfully

General Manager(P&IR)

Copy to:
1. Mr. Abhinav Kumar Srivastava.

ANNEXURE "C"

भारत कोकिंग कोल लिमिटेड
(कोल इण्डिया लिमिटेड का एक अंग)
BHARAT COKING COAL LIMITED
(A Subsidiary of Coal India Limited)

कोयला भवन
Koyla Bhawan
कोयला नगर
Koyla Nagar
धनबाद - ८२६००५
Dhanbad - 826005

पत्रांक संख्या
Ref. No. .BCCL/GM(HRD)/NIMS. RES/2011/1751

दिनांक
Date 04th.Nov....2011

TO WHOM IT MAY CONCERN

This is to certify that Mr. ABHINAV KUMAR SHRIVASTAVA
a Ph.D Research Scholar in Management of NIMS UNIVERSITY,
Shobha Nagar, Jaipur (Pin:-303121) has successfully completed his practical training on "Workers Participation in
Management in Policy Making" in our organization for six
weeks from 17 /09/2011

I wish him every success in life

(R.N.Vishwakarma)
Sr. Manager (Mining)

Sr. Mining Engineer
H R D. Department
Kalyan Bhawan, B.C.Co.

पंजिकृत कार्यालय : कोयला भवन, कोयला नगर, धनबाद।
Regd. Office : Koyla Bhawan, Koyla Nagar, Dhanbad.

ग्राम : कोकिंगकोल
Gram : KOKINGKOL

☎ : (0326) 2230133-147
☎ : (0326) 2230133-147

ANNEXURE "D(1)"

ජල සම්පාදන හා ජලාපවහන අමාතනංශය

நீர் வழங்கல் மற்றும் வடிகாலமைப்பு அமைச்சு

MINISTRY OF WATER SUPPLY AND DRAINAGE

මගේ අංකය எனது இல. My No. } 3/1/7/79	මගේ අංකය உமது இல. Your No }	දිනය திகதி Date } 06.01.2012

Mr. Abhinav Kumar Shrivastava,
PhD Research Scholar in Management
NIMS University,
ShobhaNagar, Jaipur,
India, Pin:-303121.

Reference   : - Application of Prof (Dr.) N.C.Pahariya vide "NIMSUR / Reg./ Acad/ PhD/ 2011/ PH/10/50-A"Dated 06-12-2011

Subject   : - Approval of Grant of Permission to your academic visit at Ministry of Water Supply and Drainage, Sri Lanka for Data Collection for data collection of your PhD Research Topic "Worker's Participation in Management in Policy Making".

Dear Mr. Abhinav Kumar Shrivastava,

This reference is to intimate you that request of research proposal forwarded by your PhD Thesis Supervisor, Prof.(Dr.) N.C. Pahariya vide Ref. No."NIMSUR/ Reg./Acad/ Ph.D/2011/PH/10/50-A" dated 06-12-2011 for your visit at Ministry of Water Supply and Drainage, Sri Lanka has been scrutinized and we have no objection in collecting data for the said academic exercise.

As per the request, for your project proposal we feel pleasure to intimate that we have some of the data available in our Ministry and National Water Supply and Drainage Board. However, you may have to meet some of the related officers with prior appointment to collect the data in both institutes.

Your academic visit is approved of seven working days between 30-01-2012 to 29-02-2012 at Ministry of Water Supply and Drainage, Sri Lanka. Your visit has been permitted at Ministry of Water Supply and Drainage Sri Lanka and National Water Supply and Drainage Board, for collection of data for your PhD Research Work. Please note that your research data collection shall subject to abide by the International Intellectual property laws and local related laws and regulations. After completion of your data collection for your PhD Research Work you have to

"ලක්දිය මැදුර" හි පාර්ලිමේන්තු පාර, පැලවත්ත, බත්තරමුල්ල.
35 "லக்திய மெதுர" புதிய பாராளுமன்ற வீதி, பெலவத்த, பத்தரமுல்ல.
"Lakdiya Medura" New Parliament Road, Pelawatta, Battaramulla.

| දුරකථන
தொலைபேசி
Telephone } | 011 2177240
011 2177241 | ෆැක්ස්
தொலைநகல்
Fax } 011 2177242 | E-mail secretary@watermin.gov.lk
Web www.mwsd.gov.lk |

ANNEXURE "D (2)"

mandatorily submit a detailed report of all the data collected to Ministry of Water Supply and Drainage, Sri Lanka.

Please do intimate at Secretary of the Ministry of Water Supply and Drainage, Sri Lanka of your academic visit a week before prior to your arrival at Ministry of Water Supply and Drainage, Sri Lanka.

I wish you the best for successful completion of your proposed academic visit and endeavour.

Yours faithfully,

A. Abeygunasekara
Secretary

CC:- Mr.K.L.L.Premanath, General Manager,
National Water Supply and Drainage Board of Sri Lanka – To Facilitate the candidate to
carryout the said research
data collection

ANNEXURE "E"

ජල සම්පාදන හා ජලාපවහන අමාත්‍යාංශය
நீர் வழங்கல் மற்றும் வடிகாலமைப்பு அமைச்சு
MINISTRY OF WATER SUPPLY AND DRAINAGE

| මගේ අංකය
எனது இல.
My No. | 3 / 1 / 7 / 79 | ඔබේ අංකය
உமது இல.
Your No. | | දිනය
திகதி
Date | 03.02.2012 |

TO WHOM IT MAY CONCERN

This is to certify that Mr.Abhinav Kumar Shrivastava, PhD Research Scholar In Management vide Enrollment Number "PH/10/62 of NIMS University ShobhaNagar,Jaipur,India,Pin:-303121" has successfully completed his Data Collection Work for his PhD Research Topic "Workers' Participation In Management In Policy Making" for a period of five days during 30-01-2012 to 03-02-2012 at Ministry of Water Supply and Drainage, Sri Lanka and at National Water Supply and Drainage Board of Sri Lanka.

He has submitted the detailed report to Ministry of Water Supply and Drainage, Sri Lanka, of the Data Collected for his PhD Research Topic "Workers' Participation In Management In Policy Making". He was found to be very punctual and disciplined while carrying out his Data Collection for PhD Research Work.

I congratulate him for successful completion of Data Collection for his PhD Research work. I wish him a lot of success to him in his endeavors in future

Chandika V Ethugala
Director (Development)
For Secretary
Ministry of Water Supply and Drainage

Date   :- Third Day of February,2012.
Place   :- Colombo,Sri Lanka.

'ලක්දිය මැදුර' නව පාර්ලිමේන්තු පාර, පැලවත්ත, බත්තරමුල්ල.
35 'லக்திய மெதுர' புதிய பாராளுமன்ற வீதி, பெலவத்தை, பத்தரமுல்ல.
'Lakdiya Medura' New Parliament Road, Pelawatte, Battaramulla.

| දුරකථන
தொலைபேசி
Telephone | 011 2177240
011 2177241 | ෆැක්ස්
தொலைநகல்
Fax | 011 2177242 | E-mail : secretary@watermin.gov.lk
Web : www.mwsd.gov.lk |

ANNEXURE "F"

MDRF

Management Development Research Foundation
New Delhi

This is to certify that

Mr. Abhinav Kumar Shrivastava

of NIMS University, Jaipur

presented paper titled

Graphology: A Concealed Tool for Creation and Development of Human Resource Capital

at 2nd National Conference on Human Resource Management

held on 8th April 2012

Chairman

ANNEXURE "G"

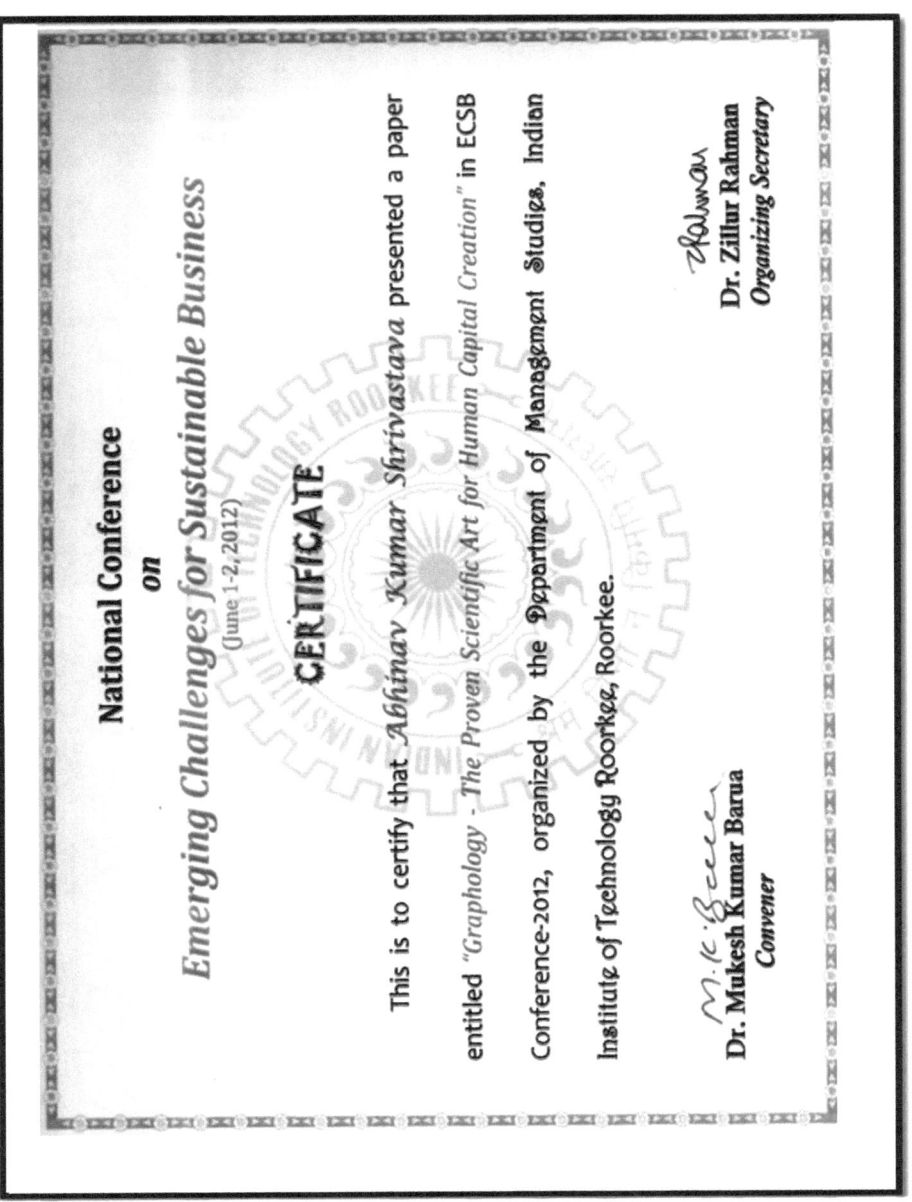

ANNEXURE "H"

INDIAN INSTITUTE OF TECHNOLOGY, DELHI

Department of Management Studies

Under the aegis of IRD

This is to certify that __**ABHINAV KUMAR SHRIVASTAVA**__ has presented a paper titled *GRAPHOLOGY:-A PROVEN SCIENTIFIC SKILL FOR IDENTIFICATION ANDNURTURING THE LEADERSHIP TRAITS.* in 2nd National Conference on **"Excellence in Higher Education"** from June 28th to 30th, 2012 at the Indian Institute of Technology, Delhi.

(Dr. Harish Chaudhry)
Conference Coordinator

(Prof. S. K. Jain)
Head, DMS

ANNEXURE "I"

HIGHER SCHOOL OF ECONOMICS
NATIONAL RESEARCH UNIVERSITY
FACULTY OF MANAGEMENT

July 5, 2012

ABHINAV KUMAR SHRIVASTAVA
PhD RESEARCH SCHOLAR IN MANAGEMENT
ENROLLMENT NUMBER: - PH/10/62
N.I.M.S. UNIVERSITY
SHOBHANAGAR, JAIPUR
INDIA,PIN:-303121

Dear Abhinav Kumar Shrivastava,

We are pleased to inform you that your paper called " Graphology: A Proven Scientific Toolkit for Perpetual Expansion of Human Resource Management Capital" is accepted for making an oral presentation at the 5th Annual Conference "Contemporary Problems in Management: Exploring the Boundaries" taking place in Moscow, Russia, Oktober, 23-24, 2012.
We would be delighted to have you present your paper at the conference.

Sincerely,

Prof. **Nikolay Filinov**

Program Committee Chair

www.ingramcontent.com/pod-product-compliance
Lightning Source LLC
Chambersburg PA
CBHW022005170526
45157CB00003B/1158